THE ART OF PEACE

21 Days To A More Peaceful You

IANN SCHONKEN

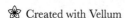

To my precious wife Melodi, and our three boys, Alexander, Christopher and Nicholas: You are my inspiration!

To my mom, Cathy: Thank you for your support and example. Thank you for introducing me to the Prince of Peace, Jesus.

To my beloved church family and readers everywhere: Let's learn how to live in peace in a hurting world!

CONTENTS

PREFACE

There are many, many possible reasons why you chose to open this book today. I honestly cannot say why you did. Maybe you are intrigued by the title. Perhaps it was a gift from someone you love or respect. Maybe you are going through a particularly difficult time in your life right now. Perhaps you are responding to a cry in your heart to find a place where you can experience peace again.

Peace seems to be in short supply in our world today. In contrast, there are always those people who seem to have an oasis of peace. No matter how bad it gets, they maintain a core of peace in the middle of their storms.

In this book, I would like to explore some ageless principles about peace. How can we have a peace that prevails regardless of the storms that assail us? I will not exhaust all the methods and strategies by which you can maintain your peace. I will do my best to provide you with enough inspiration to launch and assist you as you journey towards peace.

Why this effort to help you find peace? I wrote this book

because I have had my share of tumultuous seasons. I have had my sleepless nights. I have had lingering chest pains due to the stress of trying to figure my way through this modern life we share. As a lead pastor for almost ten years, I have lost my peace many times, trying my best to help my congregation work through their tragedies. It was hard since I struggled with my share of disappointments and setbacks.

I have listened to many sincere people, telling stories of looking for peace in all the wrong places. On my journey, I have learned that you cannot just fix people or their problems. Believe me when I say that I have tried! At best, I think I can inspire, educate and empower people. I do not believe that I can fix everything that is broken in their lives. While there are things we can do to help people, there are things they must do for themselves. There are also things that only God can do for them. The wisdom to discern the difference between those things is an essential aspect of maintaining your peace in life!

After an introduction, I explore eight perspectives on understanding and finding peace for yourself. Following that, I provided twenty-one days of training towards creating a peaceful mindset.

I suggest that you read a chapter a day for the following twenty-one days. Try to incorporate the lesson learned each day and pay attention to your levels of peace as you do. Please resist the temptation to rush ahead and finish this book in a single reading session. (Yes, you can finish it in about 3 hours.) Instead, savor the day's lesson and allow yourself to ponder its implications. Then, the next day, when you add a new layer of inspiration, you will not forget the previous day's lesson.

By the way, I have written this book with the intention of making the concept of peace as simple as possible. As you read, you may even accuse me of making things too simple at times. Please understand that the idea is to break things into smaller, simpler parts. Modern readers have limited time and busy schedules. Chapters were tailored to be short reading sessions of about 2-5 minutes each. These chapters provide a mosaic of perspectives on peace with God, self, and others.

At first, it will feel like a challenging discipline to apply these wisdom principles. Start the process, and, before long, you will break into the delight of a peaceful lifestyle. Know this: New levels of peace are possible. Learn to focus on peace and experience it every day. Thank you for reading!

Iann Schonken

UNDERSTAND THE A.R.T. OF P.E.A.C.E.

INTRODUCTION

Dr. Reinhold Niebuhr, an American theologian, wrote a simple prayer, named *The Serenity Prayer*[1]. It captures the spiritual journey towards peace beautifully. While many are familiar with the abridged version, the entire prayer is powerful and worth reading:

> *God, give us grace to accept with serenity*
> *the things that cannot be changed,*
> *Courage to change the things*
> *which should be changed,*
> *and the Wisdom to distinguish*
> *the one from the other.*
> *Living one day at a time,*
> *Enjoying one moment at a time,*
> *Accepting hardship as a pathway to peace,*
> *Taking, as Jesus did,*
> *This sinful world as it is,*
> *Not as I would have it,*

> *Trusting that You will make all things right,*
> *If I surrender to Your will,*
> *So that I may be reasonably happy in this life,*
> *And supremely happy with You forever in the next.*
> *Amen.*

— RICHARD NIEBUHR (1892–1971)

Amen indeed! Wouldn't you love it if God granted you this kind of serenity? Don't we all want to be reasonably happy in this life and supremely happy in the next? Absolutely!

Okay, what is *serenity?* *Serenity* means *being calm, peaceful, and untroubled.* I would say that most people desire to live in such a state, but the truth is that most don't. Instead, judging by what we see in the media, you would think that we are living in a dangerous society. You would believe that we are all teetering on the brink of imminent annihilation. The daily news cycle is so negative that people are anxious. I'd venture to say that many are as far removed from experiencing peace as the East is from the West!

In 2017, Neil Strauss explored the reasons for our perpetual anxiety in an October article for *Rolling Stone Magazine.* He entitled his article, *"Why We Are Living in the Age of Fear[2]."* He wondered if we should be so fearful and anxious. He started his research by asking just how unsafe it is to live in America, compared to other decades in its history.

He came across the work of Barry Glassner, one of the country's leading sociologists and author of *The Culture of Fear[3].* *Glassner* asserted that *"Most Americans are living in the safest place at the safest time in human history."*

Strauss reminds his readers that longevity, household wealth and education are on the rise. In the United States, life expectancy is higher than ever, our air is cleaner than it has been in a decade and violent crime is trending downward. *The Atlantic* reported that 2015 was *"The best year in history for the average human being.*[4]*"*

How can we be living in the safest time in human history and still be so scared at the same time? Glassner provides a clue to the mystery:

> *We are living in the most fear-mongering time in human history. And the main reason for this is that there's a lot of power and money available to individuals and organizations who can perpetuate these fears.*

Your fear is worth billions of dollars to mass media and insurance companies. You can rest assured that big pharmaceutical companies, advocacy groups, lawyers, politicians, and many others gain from your anxiety. Your fear is easy to manipulate. Think about how many *good news* stories get reported on in the media or social media. The money is in bad news, real or imagined. As long as we subscribe, watch and forward the bad news, it will perpetuate an appetite for more of the same. Inadvertently, we all feel the need to be informed so we may be safe from harm.

With all the bad news, the stress goes up, the sleep gets less, the diet goes haywire, and the frustration lingers. Our interpersonal relationships suffer as we cluster with other folks who are high on a media-fueled anxiety. Our peace is the unfortunate casualty as we squint at a horizon where imagined storm clouds gather to swallow our families. Wow! We really should stop watching so much negativity[5]!

How does a believer in God respond to this fearmongering? Many of the threats that surround us are quite real. Jesus made it clear that the enemy wants to kill, steal and destroy (John 10:10). It is my experience that those words are still valid. Look around you, and you will see that there is just so much pain everywhere. Read your history books and look back over the centuries. Hurting people throughout the ages. Even a couple of thousands of years ago, when Jesus walked the dusty roads of Palestine, the confusion and suffering were evident on the faces of the people:

> *Jesus went through all the towns and villages, teaching in their synagogues, proclaiming the good news of the kingdom and healing every disease and sickness. When he saw the crowds, he had compassion on them, because they were harassed and helpless, like sheep without a shepherd. Jesus went through all the towns and villages, teaching in their synagogues, proclaiming the good news of the kingdom and healing every disease and sickness. When he saw the crowds, he had compassion on them, because they were harassed and helpless, like sheep without a shepherd.*

> — MATTHEW 9:35-36 (NLT)

Jesus had compassion on them because He saw that they were harassed and helpless, desperately in need of a shepherd to lead them to safety. He came to be that good shepherd, and He had provided a way out of the confusion and pain for us all.

Today, while we are acutely aware that human suffering is real and proximate, we should find solace in knowing that it will come to an end at some point in the future. Jesus, in His parting instructions to His disciples, gave us some hope and inspiration:

> *I am leaving you with a gift—peace of mind and heart. And the peace I give is a gift the world cannot give. So don't be troubled or afraid. Remember what I told you: I am going away, but I will come back to you again. If you really loved*

me, you would be happy that I am going to the Father, who is greater than I am. I have told you these things before they happen so that when they do happen, you will believe.

— JOHN 14:27-29 (NLT)

I love that Jesus gives us a gift of peace! Boy, do we need that today! No matter how hard it tries, this world will never be able to give us peace. I need a peaceful state of mind. I do not want to be afraid of everything that could go wrong.

I can testify that I have enjoyed the peace of God in my life, and I can attest there is nothing quite like it. I have learned to appreciate the peace of God more than ever. I do not take peace for granted.

I do not wish to lose the peace of God because I am distracted by negative things. I want to guard the peace of God in my life so that nothing will be able to steal it from me. Unfortunately, I can have my peace stolen in an instant, even in the middle of a beautiful church service! It happened before, and it can happen again.

The enemy desires to pickpocket our peace. If he can turn our attention from the Lord of Peace to the world of turmoil, he can rob us of our faith in God. In the parable of the sower, the seed falls on different soils with different results. Jesus later explains the parable to His disciples, and as you read, look how the enemy robs us of God's blessings:

> *Now listen to the explanation of the parable about the farmer planting seeds: The seed that fell on the footpath represents those who hear the message about the Kingdom and don't understand it. Then the evil one comes and*

*snatches away the seed that was planted in their hearts. The
seed on the rocky soil represents those who hear the message
and immediately receive it with joy. But since they don't have
deep roots, they don't last long. They fall away as soon as
they have problems or are persecuted for believing God's
word. The seed that fell among the thorns represents those
who hear God's word, but all too quickly the message is
crowded out by the worries of this life and the lure of
wealth, so no fruit is produced. The seed that fell on good
soil represents those who truly hear and understand God's
word and produce a harvest of thirty, sixty, or even a
hundred times as much as had been planted!*

— MATTHEW 13:18-23 (NLT)

Interesting, isn't it? For some, the seed is snatched away. For
others, problems and persecutions divert their attention, and
they miss out. For some, it is the worries of this life and the lure
of wealth that crowd out the Word of God. The last group does
not allow anything to break their focus, and they reap the
harvest of God's increase.

Why do I share this parable here? Many believers are
anxious and without peace, because they have not been intentional in protecting their peace. I think that many are distracted
by the unsettling events of this world, and they miss out on the
harvest God had planned for them. I believe that it is possible to
be in a room with Jesus Himself and still feel void of God's
peace as you focus on the things of this world.

How is that even possible? In another biblical narrative,
Martha, a faithful supporter of Jesus, experienced this as the
Lord visited her home:

> *As Jesus and the disciples continued on their way to Jerusalem, they came to a certain village where a woman named Martha welcomed him into her home. Her sister, Mary, sat at the Lord's feet, listening to what he taught. But Martha was distracted by the big dinner she was preparing. She came to Jesus and said, 'Lord, doesn't it seem unfair to you that my sister just sits here while I do all the work? Tell her to come and help me.' But the Lord said to her, 'My dear Martha, you are worried and upset over all these details! There is only one thing worth being concerned about. Mary has discovered it, and it will not be taken away from her.'*

— LUKE 10:38-42 (NLT)

Martha lost her peace. She became worried and upset over all the details, the many things for which she was responsible. Remember the parable of the sower where it mentioned the worries of life? It happened to Martha. Is it possible that it can happen to us?

It looks like her sister Mary seemed serene and peaceful where she sat at the feet of Jesus. She had found her peace in the presence of the Lord. She paid attention to the most important person in her space, who was Jesus. When challenged, Jesus clarified that He would not allow Martha to deprive Mary of what she found in Him. With that, He set Himself up as the defender of her moment, her moment of peace with Him. I believe the Lord wants to be our Source of Peace, as much as the Defender of Peace. We must focus on Him.

Wherever your life is heading, you are going to need God's peace to overcome the obstacles while on your journey. Jesus emphasized just how important peace was to Him. Should we not consider the same for ourselves? I suggest that peace must become an integral part of our lives.

WHAT IS PEACE?

Peace is a stress-free state of security and calmness. It comes when there's no conflict, with everything coexisting in perfect harmony and freedom.

Mary experienced a state of peace at the feet of Jesus. Martha, on the other hand, was stressed-out. Both had the same options to choose from in their situation. Jesus said that Mary wanted the better part and that He will not take that from her. Martha chose the lesser part, and she suffered because of her choice.

PEACE IS... A STRESS-FREE STATE OF SECURITY AND CALMNESS...

On a daily basis, we are faced with options. We either

choose to walk in peace or add to our anxiety. Our choice, we get to choose.

Now, to be realistic, Mary's moment at the feet of Jesus did not last forever. She had to get up after a while to attend to His expressed needs. She had to move on and deal with whatever else came her way just like everybody else. Similarly, we all need to find our peace in Jesus, and then move on to serve Jesus in an adversarial world.

We must get our priorities straight so we can serve Him in the way He requires at this moment, in this hour.

Look at what Mary did. She took time to hear from Jesus by spending some time with Him. That way she had a better sense of how she may serve Him once she left her seat at His feet.

Peter wrote a letter to the early church, and it encapsulates the same principle:

> *May God give you more and more grace and peace as you grow in your knowledge of God and Jesus our Lord.*

> — 2 PETER 1:2 (NLT)

Peter wrote that growing in your knowledge of God opens you up for the blessings of God's grace and peace. Mary somehow knew that it was important to grow in her understanding of God and Jesus our Lord. She changed the pace of her day by pausing long enough to receive the grace and peace she needed to serve Him best. I pray that we will all learn this while on our journey in search of peace.

HOW DO WE RECEIVE OUR PEACE?

I will use the words *A.R.T.* and *P.E.A.C.E* as acronyms to help me explain how we could learn the art of peace. I titled this book *The Art of Peace* because I do not view our journey towards peace as a recipe or a formula. Peace is not like mathematics. Mathematics looks to arrive at a single correct answer using predictable methods. Art, on the other hand, doesn't have to *add up* or be logical to be valid or impactful. It is a process that takes time, and the journey is as important as the destination. The creator of the art piece determines what it will be, whether a poem, a song, a dance or a painting.

In 2014, I invited an artist friend, Bernie Apodaca, to come to my home and teach me how to create modern art paintings. I was feeling stuck during a very stressful season. Up to that point in my life, I did not consider myself an artist. I felt I had zero talent for creating art. Like a child, I wanted to try something different and relaxing. Little did I know what an amazing world would open to me as I entered through the door of painting and drawing! I just wanted to create colorful, modern style paintings. My friend Bernie showed up with paints and canvases at my home. We threw open the garage doors and draped a tarp over my ping-pong table. Within minutes we were off to the races! I loved every minute of it! *Voilà!* Two colorful canvases ended up on my living room wall as soon as the paint dried!

Quite frankly, I was hooked. Since then I have created many colorful canvases that are hanging on walls in my home and office. I draw and paint on paper, canvas, and glass (my *iPad Pro* with an *Apple Pencil*). I can report that it is so liberating to create without having to *add up* or *make sense*. Every piece is unique and expressive. It is liberating, and I enjoy the process as much as the result.

I find great joy in learning new skills as I add new tools year after year. I have designed the cover for this book. Also, I have included grayscale versions of some of my works throughout this book. I guess I am an enthusiastic novice!

Why ramble on about my attempts at art? All that to say this: Peace is like art in that it is a daily and unique experience. As unique as your day, so unique will be your journey towards experiencing peace in this world. Ask any classroom of kids to draw a tree with birds on its branches. You will end up with pieces of art as different as the kids that created them.

In the same way, the peace process in your life will take shape in a way as unique as you are. Some people are peaceful in one way while others are peaceful in other ways. You will find that every day will call for its own pace and rhythm. Each day will have its unique demands and expressions of peaceful service unto the Lord.

Let's lean in and enlarge our understanding of *the art of peace.*

---

1. See Reinhold Niebuhr, *"Reinhold Niebuhr: Serenity Prayer,"* Wikipedia, https://en.wikipedia.org/wiki/Reinhold_Niebuhr#Serenity_Prayer.

2. See Neill Strauss, *"Why We Are Living in the Age of Fear: This is the safest time in human history. So why are we all so afraid?"* Rolling Stone, October 6, 2016, www.rollingstone.com/politics/politics-features/why-were-living-in-the-age-of-fear-190818/

3. See Barry Glassner, *The Culture of Fear: Why Americans Are Afraid of the Wrong Things*, New York: Hachette Books, 1999).

4. See Charles Kenny, *"2015: The Best Year in History for the Average Human Being."* The Atlantic, December 18, 2015, www.theatlantic.com/international/archive/2015/12/good-news-in-2015/421200/

5. See Ryan Holiday, *"Seriously, You—Ok, We—Need To Stop Watching The News This Year."* https://ryanholiday.net/stop-watching-the-news/.

1

A.WARENESS AND ATTRACTION

> *But forget all that—it is nothing compared to what I am going to do. For I am about to do something new. See, I have already begun! Do you not see it? I will make a pathway through the wilderness. I will create rivers in the dry wasteland. The wild animals in the fields will thank me, the jackals and owls, too, for giving them water in the desert. Yes, I will make rivers in the dry wasteland so my chosen people can be refreshed.*
>
> — ISAIAH 43:18-20 (NLT)

Do you not see it? Do you not perceive it? God still speaks through the Old Testament prophet to our generation. There is a startling relevance as He questions our inattention to the obvious. We stumble past the answers, distracted. We are zombies as we stare at the screens on our walls, in our hands, and on our wrists. We have more tools to organize our lives than ever before. Yet, the chaos of our world blinds us to the reality of our peace-less existence.

We are unaware that God is already at work. He is shaping the solutions and pathways we need to take out of our troubles. He is already raining on the mountains. Streams are dancing and tumbling downhill to cut through the parched dirt of the desert. He is working to refresh our thirsty souls. We gather at the holy river in wide-eyed wonder. *How did He know? How did He do it? He came at the moment we needed Him most!*

Still many do not recognize the provision, and stumble ahead, oblivious to the oasis taking shape right next to them. Strange? Not really. It is part of the human condition to see how long we can go before we ask for help. We can be so independent at times. It seems like we have to get to the end of ourselves to realize just how dehydrated we have become. Days of running and working and buzzing around town have turned into weeks of running low on peace. When we finally run dry of peace and joy, we become acutely aware of our dryness. We desperately pant for a nectar drop of God's presence. King David writes in his song about a deer that pants for water in the wasteland, parched and desperate:

> *As the deer pants [longingly] for the water brooks, So my soul pants [longingly] for You, O God.*
>
> — PSALM 42:1 (AMP)

Isn't it funny how God often is the last one to be approached for help? We talk to our family, our friends, and strangers on Facebook, and then we finally get to God. Our desperation compels us to go to the One Who was waiting all the time. He wants to help us in a way that only He can. When Nehemiah heard about the broken-down walls of Jerusalem, he was deeply grieved and he lost his peace[1]. He cried out to God, fasting and praying for many days. He desperately reached out to God for answers. He found his answers in the presence of the Lord and his whole life changed for the better.

He was wise to recognized his need for God. God wanted his attention, and Nehemiah leaned into God for answers.

Are you finally desperate for God's peace? Recognize that He had been attracting you in many extraordinary ways. His love is drawing you, and His Spirit is calling out to you to return to His welcoming arms.

Wisdom is out on the streets, calling out to anyone who would stop long enough to listen and learn[2]. Scripture is clear that God is wise and merciful and that He runs to us when we turn towards Him. As soon as we become aware of our need for divine peace, as soon as we turn towards Him, He will move towards us:

> *Come close to God, and God will come close to you.*

> — JAMES 4:8A (NLT)

In Him, you will find the answer to your desperation. He

gives acceptance, forgiveness, healing, restoration, and hope for the future.

The Lord has been at work, but you did not perceive it. You could not discern it, because you were still too busy to see God at work around you and on your behalf. The awareness of your need for peace, and your willingness to respond to the attraction of God's love, are crucial when you are ready to grow in peace.

Next, we need to understand the importance of responding and reaching for the gift He is offering.

God's Angel Working In The Chaos, Undetected. (Acrylic paint on canvas by Iann Schonken, 2014)

REVIEW: THE A.R.T. OF P.E.A.C.E.

- A.wareness and Attraction.

---

1. See Nehemiah 1:1-11.
2. See Proverbs 1:22-33.

2

R.ESPONDING AND REACHING

'Before they call I will answer; while they are still speaking I will hear. The wolf and the lamb will feed together, and the lion will eat straw like the ox, and dust will be the serpent's food. They will neither harm nor destroy on all my holy mountain,' says the Lord.

— ISAIAH 65: 24-25 (NIV)

As soon as we realize our need for God's peace and as we recognize the draw of His Holy Spirit in our hearts, we need to respond and reach for Him. It is clear from the quotation above that God declared Himself quick to respond as we reach out to Him. How many become aware of their thirst for the divine impartation of peace, who acknowledge that they sense God wooing them, yet, sadly, turn away. Their heads are down because they feel that reaching out to God will be met with rejection.

We often feel so far away from God that reaching out to God for help seems like an impossible task. We pant and crave a sip from the cup of living water, but our insecurities cry out, *"Don't respond! Don't reach out! God will never take you back!"*

God declared through his spokesman Isaiah that He is vigilantly awaiting our cry for help.

God is a gentleman Who gave us our freedom to choose. He will not force Himself on us, not even in moments of weakness. However, when He sees us open our mouths to cry for help, He will rush to our side with the answer we need to find the peace we so desire.

How powerful the imagery of the wolf, the lamb, and the lion, peacefully next to each other without fear or trepidation. That is the kind of peace the Lord the Lord has in mind for us. He is just waiting for us to move towards Him!

I am reminded of Jesus' parable of the lost son, coming to his senses and returning to his father's house after shamefully squandering his inheritance. When the father saw his son approaching, he ran out to meet him. He embraced him and ordered clean clothes and new sandals. A party was hastily put together, and neighbors were invited over to celebrate his return.

Can you imagine the feeling of putting his feet under his father's table, which was laden with the finest foods and drinks, after having been living a miserable existence in a pig sty? What was it like to lay his head on a clean pillow, with fresh linens, in a house where he could feel safe and at peace?

In the same way, when we feel that we are parched and harassed by life, we can respond and reach out to the Lord. He will not reject us, but He will rush to embrace us with His incredible love. God's provision and His peace will replace the anxiety and trepidation so evident in our lives, and we will be able to enjoy the bounty at His table. However, without responding and reaching, we stay in a state of deprivation. Apart from God, we remain anxious and far removed from God's blessings and protection.

We get to choose where we get to spend our lives. I want to invite you to come close to God. Respond and reach for God. Whisper a simple prayer:

> *Lord, please help me. I am sorry for my failed efforts. Please be my Lord and Savior, Jesus. Fill me with your Holy Spirit and show me how to live in peace. I am all yours, Lord.*

God will respond and come close to you. You may not see Him, but you will feel the warmth of His loving acceptance and affirmation. His peace will fill you to overflowing!

Next, we need to understand the importance of transmitting the good news of what we have experienced in God's presence.

REVIEW: THE A.R.T. OF P.E.A.C.E.

- A.wareness and Attraction.
- R.esponding and Reaching.

3

T.RANSMIT

> *To me, art is just as tangible as it is intangible. It is both the emotion and intention behind any given piece as well as the piece itself. Art is something you invest yourself in as a means to communicate. It can be the most beautiful thing in the entire world as well as the most horrific. It all depends on the artist.*
>
> — CHRISTIAN VILLANUEVA, DISNEY
> PERFORMER, AND YOUTUBE ARTIST

When we encounter the peace of God, it is usually a powerful and beautiful experience. As a result, we will feel the need to share that peace with others. Some folks write poems, songs, or create paintings. Others share a smile of peaceful contentment with the people they encounter during the day.

Humans are social and find expression for how they feel on

the inside by talking about it. Emotional states are reflected in people's work or creativity.

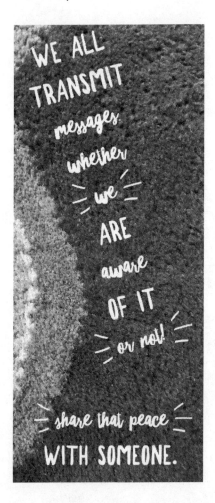

We communicate a myriad of messages about the state of our inner peace to the world around us.

We do the same when we experience sadness or anxiety. We are like a television attached to a satellite dish. The receiver is tuned to a channel of the frequencies transmitted by the satellite. As it downloads the data, it displays the images and emits the sounds of the selected channel. Likewise, as humans, we choose the channel we desire to tune into, and we receive that signal. We display what we have received from that selection on our faces and in our body language. If we have chosen to be tuned into what is harmful and toxic, we will end up displaying negativity as others look at us and listen to our words. If we have decided to be tuned into what is positive and uplifting, we will display happier faces and speak more edifying words.

We cannot help but transmit what we have allowed to fill us up. Sometimes I come home wrestling with an issue from my day at work. Inevitably, my wife will pick up something is off and ask me what is wrong. I did not say anything to give her a clue regarding my anxiety. How did she know? She picked up that I have somehow lost my peace. I couldn't help transmitting it in my countenance, my posture, and my silence.

We must become aware that we are transmitters of both peace and anxiety. We have to become intentional. We must make sure that we download peaceful and wholesome messages into our hearts:

 And now, dear brothers and sisters, one final thing. Fix your thoughts on what is true, and honorable, and right, and pure, and lovely, and admirable. Think about things that are excellent and worthy of praise. Keep putting into practice all you learned and received from me—everything you heard from me and saw me doing. Then the God of peace will be with you.

— PHILIPPIANS 4:8-9 (NLT)

When we fix our thoughts on the right stuff, we will have positive outcomes. The adage of *"garbage in, garbage out,"* comes to mind. The question is, what do you generally communicate in your work, your words, your posture, and your countenance? We cannot expect to transmit hope and peace into the world when we feast on the negativity of talk radio and the internet.

We can create and transmit beautiful or horrific art with our lives. I desire to create beauty and hope in the world. When we realize our need for peace, and as we respond to God's attraction by reaching out to Him, He will begin to download His peace into our lives. As we stay tuned into God's presence, we will start to transmit (or communicate) that fantastic peace and joy to others. I believe it will be in a way that will be as unique as each one of us. Expect people to resonate with how you reflect the peaceful nature of God. As they ask you about what makes you different, you can use those opportunities to introduce them to the God of Peace.

We all transmit messages, whether we realize it or not. We all produce art with our thoughts, words, and actions. We all get to live lives that could either uplift others or drag them down. We all get to choose what it will be, regardless of our circumstances.

REVIEW: THE A.R.T. OF P.E.A.C.E.

- A.wareness and Attraction.
- R.esponding and Reaching.
- T.ransmit.

4

P.RIORITIES

> *There is a time for everything, and a season for every activity under the heavens:*

— ECCLESIASTES 3:1 (NIV)

Because we are all different, we will have different priorities on a given day. I believe that Mary's story at the feet of Jesus provides us with some clues to help us[1]. She chose to do only one thing, namely to sit at the feet of Jesus and to listen to Him. She prioritized that one thing and made it her focus. Martha tried to shame her sister Mary for that chosen priority, but Jesus disagreed. He confirmed that Mary's choice was wise.

I believe that if peace is a priority in your life, you will have to get a firm grip on your preferences.

What is a priority? A priority is something that is considered more important than another. Mary decided that time with

Jesus was more important than doing a series of tasks in the kitchen. She was right. Martha was wrong.

Here is a clue to help you find more peace in your life: Whenever things start to spin out of control, ask yourself *The Priority Question:*

> *What is the one thing I should be doing right now?*

In our world, we feel validated by checking a lot of stuff off our to-do lists. Too often we are majoring in the minor things of life. We should do less of those small things, those unimportant things. Instead, we must try our best to do the right thing at the right time.

Ask yourself the following questions when your peace seems absent:

- What should I be doing right now?
- This hour?
- Today?

Don't let petty things, foolish pursuits and other people's *important* become your *urgent*. When you know your priority, it must become your singular focus.

FOCUS: FOLLOW ONE COURSE UNTIL SUCCESS

Later today, as your peace ebbs away, you may lament that you don't know what your priority should be. When that happens, take a deliberate step to enter God's presence. Find a spot to pray and get an audience with the Lord! It is not that hard. Go to the restroom, close the door and breathe a simple prayer. God is listening and ready to meet you where you are.

Next, let's explore some thoughts on entering God's presence.

REVIEW: THE A.R.T. OF P.E.A.C.E.

- A.wareness and Attraction.
- R.esponding and Reaching.
- T.ransmit
- P.riorities

---

1. See Luke 10:38-42 (NLT).

5

E.NTER HIS PRESENCE

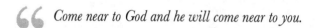 *Come near to God and he will come near to you.*

— JAMES 4:8 (NIV)

Mary understood that she needed to stop and pay attention to Jesus first. She moved Jesus into the center of her focus. She understood that by listening and learning, she would be able to figure out where she needed to spend her energy and resources to serve Jesus.

Likewise, in our days, we should:

- Talk to the Lord when we can, wherever we can.
- Forgive those who have harmed us. (Don't allow others to steal your peace and blessings.)
- Regain our peace in His reassuring presence.
- Declare our willingness to be used this day in any way necessary.
- Ask the Lord for His priorities.

- Get your priorities in line with God's will.

A rigid prioritized schedule may push people off your radar who God may want you to help. *The parable of the Good Samaritan* provides a great example to us[1]. The priest is going to the temple. Looks like the right priority right? However, when he sees an injured man on the side of the road, he passes him without offering to help. Why? There are many possible reasons. One of them may be that he was so focused on where he was going that he couldn't see the need of the man on the side of the road.

We have all been in that place of hurry and *tunnel vision*. In contrast, the Samaritan is willing to abandon his priority temporarily. He responds to the broken, hurting individual who is God's revealed priority at that moment. We must always remember that while priorities are important, you may have a wrong priority! Choosing your own priority over God's priority is way too easy! Check in with God as you go along. You will be surprised by what can happen to your priorities.

Jesus is our example in this regard. He allowed people to interrupt Him. When He sensed His Father was calling on Him to pause alongside someone, He did. Jesus' willingness to adjust benefited Bartimaeus, Zaccheus, and the woman with the hemorrhage. We must become like Jesus in our willingness to adjust in the moment to an instruction from Holy Spirit. That requires a surrendered heart and a flexibility to the progressively revealed will of the Lord.

I believe that entering the presence of God is not just a scheduled meeting at the beginning of the day. It is not just a rite, ritual or religious discipline. Rather, it is a continual inner conversation with God that keeps the heart's door open to updates and divine insights. How is that possible? By involving God in everything that happens to you and around you.

We enter His presence by inviting Him into our inner world throughout the day. I call these *"burst communications"* with God. Ask God for help, wisdom, or direction in short bursts of mental prayer. Instead of long, rambling prayers, make them short and sweet.

That's how we can enter God's presence throughout the day without having to make a church service out of it. You don't need an orchestra playing the right songs to get you in the right mindset. You don't need a preacher with a sermon. That's what you do on Sunday, but today is today and you may be far away from a church building.

God is there, with you, right now. Just talk to Him under your breath, or in your mind. There is no need to kneel, or to withdraw from others. You can engage with God in a way nobody will even know about. Right there in the meeting with your boss or coworker, talk to God in your thoughts. Sometimes, when I feel my anxiety rising I breathe a simple prayer: "Lord, I need your wisdom. Please help me in this situation."

ENTER HIS
presence
YOUR PEACE IS GROWING!

It usually doesn't take long before His peace settles in and solutions start to emerge. You can enter His presence by inviting Him into your prayerful thoughts. You will be surprised how quickly you can get the peace you need to make the right decisions throughout the day. His presence is a deliberate thought away. Talk to Him right now. He is waiting with the answers to your questions.

Next, let's look at the access you give people and how it may affect your peace.

REVIEW: THE A.R.T. OF P.E.A.C.E.

- A.wareness and Attraction.
- R.esponding and Reaching.
- T.ransmit.
- P.riorities.
- E.nter His Presence.

---

1. Luke 10:25-37.

6

A.CCESS

❝❝ *Do not be deceived: 'Evil company corrupts good habits.'*

— I CORINTHIANS 15:33 (NKJV)

While we are to be open to the Lord's guidance in helping people along the way, we must pay close attention to whom we give access! We all are aware that one conversation with a particular individual (*you know the one!*) can drain your peace. The truth is that when you give the wrong people access to you, it creates an adverse domino effect in your life. By the time they exit your presence, you feel like a wrung-out rag, devoid of energy and drained of vitality. Each one of us has to become more vigilant to track and manage who has access to our lives.

A person who serves as a great example in managing access is Nehemiah. Nehemiah (a prominent figure in Jewish history) was in the middle of his project to rebuild the walls of Jerusalem. There were enormous pressures and opposition to the project, and many people wanted it to fail. They knew that if they could distract or eliminate Nehemiah, the project would falter.

> *Sanballat and Geshem sent word to me, saying, 'Come, let us meet together at Chephirim in the plain of Ono.' But they were planning to harm me. So I sent messengers to them, saying, 'I am doing a great work and cannot come down. Why should the work stop while I leave to come down to [meet with] you?' They sent word to me four times in this way, and I answered them in the same way.*

— NEHEMIAH 6:2-4 (AMP)

Nehemiah knew what God wanted him to do. He spent a lot of time in prayer. His priority was set. Nobody was going to deter or distract him from rebuilding those walls. As a result, his focus paid off, the plot to kill him failed, and those massive walls were rebuilt in a mere 52 days!

Like Nehemiah, we must recognize that when we allow inappropriate access to people, we miss out on the peace and purposes of God. Inappropriate access leads to other people's agendas. Observe as the dominoes begin to fall, one after another, in such situations. Those agendas turn into demands that try to take over our divine priorities. Demanding expectations will soon receive more attention than warranted and multiple distractions will emerge. A scattered focus will result in frustrating delays. Compromised outcomes will result in anxiety, and a lost sense of peace.

I have seen this over and over! People with important work for God allow others to walk into their lives and distract them.

These men and women of God see the very life sucked out of their dreams and destinies. They did not control access and the *wrong people* turned into *emotional vampires*. Because of *emotional vampires*, many good people have been sucked dry of their divine destiny, and they floundered as a result!

People often lack a sense of purpose for their existence. While that is understood, it does not mean you have to drop everything to coddle their besetting issues. Sitting around sipping tea only to rehash their bad decisions for the past decade? No way! I'm sure other people love doing that, but we should refuse living like that unless you are a counselor with the calling and skills to help people in that situation.

BEWARE! EMOTIONAL VAMPIRES

Do not allow anyone to steal hours out of your life if they don't have respect for your God-given priorities. Also, stay out of other people's political arguments and religious controversies[1]. Those conversations are nothing but bottomless swamps. Stay away from them.

Do not give people access to the grace and peace God had deposited in your life. Instead, guard your peace with great determination! I refuse to respond to people who send me angry comments in texts, emails and on social media. I have figured out that I cannot fix most of the world's problems. I have also learned that unless God had assigned me to address a specific issue, I would most likely lose my peace over it if I am not care-ful. My cause in life is too important to be sidelined by the wrong people. Likewise, your cause in life is too important to give access to the wrong people. Put a guard at the door to your life. You will be glad you did.

Next, let's consider how staying true to your cause creates peace in your life.

REVIEW: THE A.R.T. OF P.E.A.C.E.

- A.wareness and Attraction.
- R.esponding and Reaching.
- T.ransmit.
- P.riorities.
- E.nter His Presence.
- A.ccess.

---

1. See Titus 3:9.

C.AUSE

So many people lose their peace because they forgot their cause. By *cause* I mean their *why*. Their cause is their *purpose*, their *zeal* and *reason* for *being and doing* as they live their lives. When you have a strong cause, or *why*, you are not easily distracted by what others are doing or thinking. You don't have the time to give your focus to everyone else's theories or anxieties. Even the storms of life shouldn't deter you because they are merely obstacles on the way to a great future accomplishment. Having an important *why* in your life is essential. Otherwise, someone else's purpose will determine your future.

We must all try to keep our individual causes crystal clear. We must have a well-developed sense of our assignments as we spend our lives here on earth. There are many excellent resources available to assist you in figuring out your purpose in life. Every one of us should do our best to figure out our cause, and then we should periodically evaluate whether we are still on track.

When we pursue our God-given causes, we bring glory to God, our Lord and Creator. Ultimately, we are *all* called to bring glory to God with our lives:

66 *Everything comes from God alone. Everything lives by his power, and everything is for his glory.*

— ROMANS 11:36 (LB)

In the end, we will all give an account of our lives to God. In the Gospel of Matthew, in the twenty-fifth chapter, Jesus told three parables of accountability. In the first, He painted the picture of the five foolish and five wise virgins. Five were ready for His return, and five were not.

Second, He told the *parable of the talents*, reminding everyone that there will be an accounting given for our efforts here on earth. God expects us to show an increase in His investment in us.

Third, in the *parable of the sheep and the goats*, He revealed that what we do to the least of those we encounter, we have done unto Him personally. These three parables remind us that our causes and assignments in life are to be taken seriously. In the end, God desires to reward us for our contributions and how they brought glory to His Name.

Each one of us has an inborn sense of wanting to make a valuable contribution. When our lives flounder and we become adrift in a sea of fruitless activity, our sense of peace begins to wane. I call that waning sense of peace a *divine dissatisfaction,* a sense that we are off course and in need of realignment.

There are people we must reach who are sick, hungry, and in prison. There are children to be raised, inspired, educated, empowered and released into the adult world with a sense of destiny. Maybe we cannot reach everyone, but are we diligent to reach and positively impact the ones God has placed in front of us?

A sense of peace is an important indicator to let us know whether we are doing the right thing at the right time for the right reasons. The absence of peace let us know when we are adrift. Please pay attention to your cause. It is critical to your peace.

Next, we will explore the roles your energy and different environments play in maintaining your peace.

REVIEW: THE A.R.T. OF P.E.A.C.E.

- A.wareness and Attraction.
- R.esponding and Reaching.
- T.ransmit.
- P.riorities.
- E.nter His Presence.
- A.ccess.
- C.ause.

8

E.NERGY AND ENVIRONMENTS

" *When he was at the table with them, he took bread, gave thanks, broke it and began to give it to them. Then their eyes were opened and they recognized him, and he disappeared from their sight. They asked each other, 'Were not our hearts burning within us while he talked with us on the road and opened the Scriptures to us?'*

— LUKE 24:30-32 (NIV)

H ave you noticed that certain people and places seem to energize you, while others drain you? Some environments seem to have the ability to make you feel alive, alert and aligned with your cause. Other settings are frustrating. You feel awkward in your skin, and you want to run away. It is critical to your peace to be aware of how certain environments affect your energy.

I feel a considerable depletion of energy in environments where people are arguing. They seem invigorated by the exchange while I cannot get out of there quick enough! I also have noticed that I get my energy from being alone. Since I know that, I now create times during my day where I can be alone. I don't need hours alone, but those moments alone enable me to be more peaceful when I find myself in the midst of others.

Paying attention to your energy levels will help you maintain the right balance in your day. This will result in more peace in your life. Everyone is different. My wife Melodi loves time with people, and it boosts her energy and sense of peace. She will leave a social event lit up with joy. She replenishes her energy in a people-filled environment. As they say, different strokes for different folks. The key is to be aware of how environments impact your energy and peace. Make sure that you pay attention to your *Peace-O-Meter*.

| *What does your Peace-O-Meter tell you today?*

What is a *Peace-O-Meter*? It is my made-up word, but it is that internal sense of peace in your moments with people in particular places. Like a thermometer, your *Peace-O-Meter* tells you when your peace is high and when it gets low. It reveals that a particular person or a specific place is depleting your peace. I know that being in nature with beautiful trees and a lake in the distance can help me regain some peace. I also know that being around cantankerous people can steal my peace.

Pay attention to your environments. Ask yourself if a particular environment is energizing or depleting you. It is important to manage your energy and guard your peace. Energy is a resource that usually becomes depleted within a 24-hour day. We must sleep enough. Recreation is super important. Our diet is important.

I think Jesus lived with an acute awareness of His environments and His energy levels. Jesus knew when to withdraw from the crowds. Jesus slept on the boats as they traveled from shore to shore. Jesus prayed early in the morning and late at night. Jesus was able to maintain a rigorous traveling and teaching schedule. He knew to retreat, rest, and refresh Himself in prayer. He pursued His cause by setting His priorities and engaging each day with energy and peace.

If you read the Gospels, you will see that Jesus often changed environments to reset His energy. This helped me to do better. I realized that, if I don't watch my energy and environments, I will struggle to minister from a place of peace. Now, I know that there is a pace, a rhythm to life that I need to pay attention to unless I want to crash and burn.

I wanted to make sure I write about the importance of pacing ourselves as we go through our days. Life is not a sprint, but a marathon, and we need to P.A.C.E. ourselves by having the right ...

- **P**.*riorities*
- **A**.*ccess To Our Lives*
- **C**.*ause*
- **E**.*nergy and Environment*

I realized that you could not get your **P.A.C.E.** right without **E**ntering His Presence throughout your day! For the right PACE, we will have to **E**.*nter His Presence* and obtain **P.E.A.C.E.!**

I know people whose frenetic pace causes stress and sleepless nights. They don't have a daily encounter with God to bring everything into the right balance. I challenge you to read the four Gospels and find Jesus rushing anywhere! He paced His life exceptionally well. Even emergencies did not phase Him. For example, at hearing the news of Lazarus' sickness and subsequent death, He was not as disturbed as His disciples expected Him to be[1]. At another tie, He peacefully slept on a boat which was going through a frightening storm on the Sea of Galilee[2].

Jesus operated from a place of peace regardless of circumstances because He had that unbroken connection with His Father. He displayed peace at His trial. Somehow, He was not anxious. Pontius Pilate, the Proconsul, was utterly amazed. Any other human being would have been stressed-out and fearful. Jesus wasn't anxious. Why?

On the night before that important trial, Jesus took the time to enter God's presence in the Garden of Gethsemane[3]. He went there to determine His Father's priority for Him. He faced His adversaries with a peace that passed all understanding!

I have found that peace is harder to come by on some days than others. I am convinced that we can all have peace in our storms. Jesus is our example. Some of my storms have lasted for hours, days, weeks, months, and even years. The Lord always calmed me sufficiently to receive the wisdom I needed for that situation. I found that the key is to call on Him when the pace of life threatens to throw me into a ditch by the side of the road.

Remember, Jesus issued a fantastic invitation to everyone in need of peace:

> *Then Jesus said, 'Come to me, all of you who are weary and carry heavy burdens, and I will give you rest. Take my yoke upon you. Let me teach you, because I am humble and gentle at heart, and you will find rest for your souls. For my yoke is easy to bear, and the burden I give you is light.'*
>
> — MATTHEW 11:28 (NLT)

We all are living in a world that is more confusing than ever as we try to adjust to all the changes around us. Technological advancements in the last 30 years have us all hard-pressed to catch up! It is disruptive and distressing. We all have great family and career responsibilities, and they leave us weary at times. Jesus' invitation still stands. He can teach us how to be at rest in a disturbing world.

I titled this book ***The Art of Peace*** because art is as unique as the artist. It has a signature look, and the influence of the art teacher is recognizable in the student's works. In the same way, your journey towards peace in life will be uniquely yours. As you walk with Jesus, He will teach you, and there will be peace in your heart. The results of His peace in your life will manifest in beautiful, colorful ways that will bring glory to God. The journey of life will be an adventure. The pace of your life will be graced with wonderful experiences as you look to encounter God in the details of your days.

The Crazy Pace of the Big City (Acrylics on Canvas, by Iann Schonken, 2014)

I pray that you take the next twenty-one days to learn a few more things from the Bible about peace. I pray that you will no longer allow anything to rob you of the gift Jesus left each one of us: a peace that passes all understanding! May the peace of God guard your hearts and your minds in Christ Jesus. Finally, share that peace with others you encounter along the way. It will make our world a better place!

REVIEW: THE A.R.T. OF P.E.A.C.E.

- A.wareness and Attraction.
- R.esponding and Reaching.
- T.ransmit.
- P.riorities.
- E.nter His Presence.
- A.ccess.
- C.ause.
- E.nergy and Environments.

---

1. See John 11:1-44.
2. See Matthew 8:23-27.
3. Matthew 26:36 and Mark 14:32.

21 DAYS TO A MORE PEACEFUL YOU

1

GOD IS A GOD OF PEACE

> *For God is not a God of disorder but of peace, as in all the meetings of God's holy people.*

> — I CORINTHIANS 14:33 (NLT)

I want you to imagine what heaven may look like right now. Do you believe it to be a place of chaos and disorder? Do you imagine the Throne Room of the Lord filled with angels running around all stressed-out? Do you see the Lord anxiously scratching His head, confused what to do next? Or do you imagine a place of order, peace, and tranquility?

Our scripture today states that God is a God of peace, and not disorder. Peace is freedom from disturbance, a state of quiet and tranquility. It is freedom from war or violence.

Now let's consider our world and the news we can watch on the television or the events we read about on the internet. Would you believe our society to be one devoid of war and violence? A place of quiet and tranquility? I'd say, "No way!"

If God is a God of peace, then I want to invite Him into every moment of my days. Peace, for the most part, is absent from our world. Our world is noisy, violent, and filled with adversity and contention. Anyone who can bring a sense of peace to it should be welcomed.

In the scripture referenced above, Paul was trying to get his audience to understand that disorganization and discord were to be avoided in the gatherings of the church. The God of Peace was right there with them. He assumed that they would get aligned with God. He expected God's peaceful presence to permeate the atmosphere of every meeting they had. The fact that he needed to address this matter suggests that the members of the early church struggled at times to peacefully co-exist.

I have earlier discussed the story of Jesus visiting the home of Lazarus and his two sisters, Mary and Martha[1]. He arrived, and Martha came out of the kitchen, scowling and rebuking Mary for not helping with the preparations. It was pretty insulting. It broke the tranquility of the moment and disturbed the peace in the room. Martha was sincere in her desire to please the Lord, but she went about it the wrong way.

If she took a little more time in the Lord's presence, she might have had a better idea of what He needed. Jesus said that Mary chose the better option and that He could not fault her for that.

Today, decide to welcome the God of Peace into your moments and meetings. Talk to Him about every problem that may rob you of your peace, your tranquility and serenity. Put Him is charge and line your emotions and actions up with what you know will please Him. Right now, invite the Lord into your anxiety and conflicts. Soon you will feel a sense of His peaceful presence, permeating your situation.

HAVE YOU EVER
BEEN SINCERE AND WRONG
SIMULTANEOUSLY?

May the Lord of peace himself give you peace at all times and in every way. The Lord be with all of you.

— 2 THESSALONIANS 3:16 (NLT)

ACTION STEPS:

1. **Stop** what you are doing for a moment.
2. Stop fussing and thinking about what agitates you right now.
3. **Look** to the Lord and talk to Him in prayer. Talk to Him about your concerns.
4. **Listen** to His still, calming voice.
5. End your conversation by asking Him to give you His peace that passes all understanding.

6. Repeat this process whenever you feel conflicted today: Stop. Look. Listen.

7. Remember, God is a God of Peace.

REVIEW:

1. God is a God of Peace.

---

1. See Luke 10:38-42.

2

JESUS GAVE US PEACE WITH THE FATHER

> *Therefore, since we have been made right in God's sight by faith, we have peace with God because of what Jesus Christ our Lord has done for us.*

— ROMANS 5:1 (NLT)

Jesus bridged the gap between you and God. He came to earth and died for our sins. It was a gift. As we put our faith in Jesus, we receive the gift of God's forgiveness. We can return to God's family table to have communion with the Lord. That means we have a brand new identity in Christ. The old feelings of guilt can be left behind for good.

Sadly, for many people, it is tough to let those old feelings of condemnation go. They feel uneasy and stressed out whenever they try to talk to God. To them, it still feels like God can turn on them at any moment to judge or reject them. According to Henri Nouwen (an author and theologian), some of those feelings come from lies many believers still believe about their identities[1]:

1. I am what I own.
2. I am what I do.
3. I am what other people say or think about me.
4. I am nothing more than my worst moment to date.
5. I am nothing less than my best moment to date.

It is impossible to live at peace with God and yourself when you believe such lies about who you are. It is impossible because you cannot ever feel like you have enough, do enough, be liked enough, or be good enough to earn God's favor.

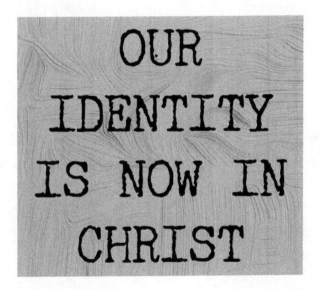

Truthfully, our identity as believers is now in Christ, and not our efforts or possessions. When Father God looks at each one of us, His children, He sees Who Jesus is and what Jesus did, and it satisfies His perfect standards. Paul wrote to the Roman church that there is no condemnation for those who are in Christ Jesus[2]. Because of what Jesus did for us, we are free to feel the peace that now exists between God and us. It is no longer about our performance, but our acceptance of His provision in Christ Jesus. Subsequently, we are empowered in our new identity to think right, speak right and do right.

I pray that you will sense and embrace the peace that signifies the ending of hostilities between God and man. Don't buy the lies of the enemy. He is attempting to separate you from your true identity in Christ. Remember, God loves you. Be still, be at peace! Become convinced of and secure in God's love for you.

   And I am convinced that nothing can ever separate us from God's love. Neither death nor life, neither angels nor demons, neither our fears for today nor our worries about tomorrow— not even the powers of hell can separate us from God's love.

— ROMANS 8:38-39 (NLT)

ACTION STEPS:

1. Look at the list of five lies we tell ourselves about our identities.
2. Do you sometimes fall into the trap of believing one of those lies?
3. How does it make you feel? Peaceful or conflicted at times?
4. Remind yourself today that God loves you. Nothing can separate you from God's enduring love.
5. Be still. Be at peace. God loves you.

REVIEW:

1. God is a God of Peace.
2. Jesus Gave Us Peace With The Father.

---

1. Excerpted on Twitter by Henri Nouwen from his Audible audiobook entitled: *"Who Are We? Reclaiming our Christian Identity."* (https://twitter.com/HenriNouwen/status/1023714857219186688).
2. See Romans 8:1.

3

WHERE GOD RULES PEACE IS EVIDENT

> *For a child is born to us, a son is given to us. The government will rest on his shoulders. And he will be called: Wonderful Counselor, Mighty God, Everlasting Father, Prince of Peace.*

— ISAIAH 9:6 (NLT)

When Isaiah prophesied about Jesus' birth, he made it clear that Jesus will be our *Prince of Peace.* Many centuries later, Jesus was born. He started His public ministry by preaching and teaching about the Kingdom of God. Jesus made it clear to His audience what it looks like when God is in charge of our lives. He admonished people to seek first the Kingdom of God and His righteousness. He explained that all the things people generally lose their peace over would be added to their lives[1].

Jesus was very intentional to teach people about the Kingdom of God. He wanted them to see the contrast between where God rules and where He does not. At the end of His earthly ministry, Jesus spent some time to focus on the issue of peace.

> *'I am leaving you with a gift—peace of mind and heart. And the peace I give is a gift the world cannot give. So don't be troubled or afraid. Remember what I told you: I am going away, but I will come back to you again. If you really loved me, you would be happy that I am going to the Father, who is greater than I am. I have told you these things before they happen so that when they do happen, you will believe.'*

> — JOHN 14:27-29 (NLT)

The Prince of Peace left His followers with the gift of peace. He told them not to be afraid of what was happening around them. Paul, the apostle, picked up the same theme in his writings to the Roman church. He reminded them that God's Kingdom is a peaceful kingdom:

> *For the Kingdom of God is not a matter of what we eat or drink, but of living a life of goodness and peace and joy in the Holy Spirit.*

> — ROMANS 14:17 (NLT)

I know that I want to live a life of goodness, peace, and joy in the Holy Spirit. I don't want to go through today with my heart troubled and afraid. I can only imagine that you would want the same kind of life. Why don't you ask Holy Spirit to help you and your family to live a life of goodness, peace, and joy? Let's agree to live a life where God is in charge so that He can bring about those desirable qualities. Where God rules, peace will be evident. Jesus made sure to leave the gift of peace to His followers on earth.

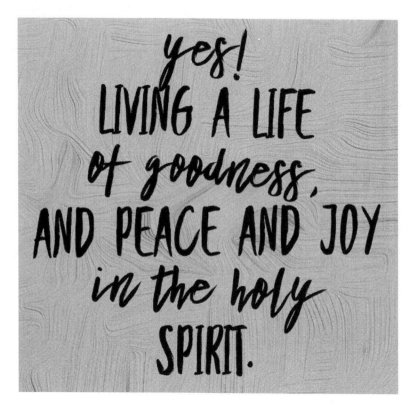

Finally, Job provided us with a caution that we will do well to remember:

> *Submit to God, and you will have peace; then things will go well for you. Listen to his instructions, and store them in your heart.*

— JOB 22:21-22 (NLT)

Will you surrender to God? If you surrender to Him, you can have the peace you desire.

ACTION STEPS:

1. Are you feeling troubled and afraid about some things?
2. Remind yourself that Jesus came and left us the gift of peace.
3. Holy Spirit can empower us to live a good life, a peaceful life.
4. Why don't you take a moment to talk to the Lord about your situation? Ask Him to rule and reign as King over those troubling details you face right now.
5. You will be so much more peaceful if you can trust Him to help *you*!

REVIEW:

1. God is a God of Peace.
2. Jesus Gave Us Peace With The Father.
3. Where God Rules Peace Is Evident.

---

1. See Matthew 6:33.

4

LET HOLY SPIRIT CONTROL YOUR MIND

> *So letting your sinful nature control your mind leads to death.*
> *But letting the Spirit control your mind leads to life*
> *and peace.*

— ROMANS 8:6 (NLT)

Take a moment and pay attention to the kind of topics you were thinking about for the last ten minutes. Did you think thoughts that inspire and encourage? Or, were they thoughts of despair, and doubt? Did you think uplifting and positive thoughts, or were you looking at the downside of your situation? Are you thinking of ways to please God or are you trying to get out of obeying the Word of God? Paul continued and clarified his train of thought in this way:

> *For the sinful nature is always hostile to God. It never did*
> *obey God's laws, and it never will. That's why those who*
> *are still under the control of their sinful nature can never*

please God. But you are not controlled by your sinful nature. You are controlled by the Spirit if you have the Spirit of God living in you.

— ROMANS 8:7-9 (NLT)

It's impossible to be at peace when you are at war with the will of God for your life.

It is impossible to be at peace when you are at war with God's will for your life. Daily, Holy Spirit teaches us to obey God's will and to become more like Him. Our sinful human natures are selfish and want to dethrone God in our thoughts, words, and actions. Elsewhere, Paul contrasted what our sinful natures produce and what Holy Spirit produces:

" *When you follow the desires of your sinful nature, the results are very clear: sexual immorality, impurity, lustful pleasures, idolatry, sorcery, hostility, quarreling, jealousy, outbursts of anger, selfish ambition, dissension, division, envy, drunkenness, wild parties, and other sins like these. Let me tell you again, as I have before, that anyone living that sort of life will not inherit the Kingdom of God. But the Holy Spirit produces this kind of fruit in our lives: love, joy, peace, patience, kindness, goodness, faithfulness, gentleness, and self-control. There is no law against these things! Those who belong to Christ Jesus have nailed the passions and desires of their sinful nature to his cross and crucified them there. Since we are living by the Spirit, let us follow the Spirit's leading in every part of our lives. Let us not become conceited, or provoke one another, or be jealous of one another.*

— GALATIANS 5:19-26 (NLT)

Let's ask Holy Spirit to produce the right kind of thinking in us by taking control of our thoughts. When Holy Spirit controls our minds, the results are peaceful, joyful and enduring.

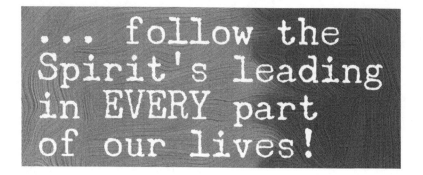
... follow the Spirit's leading in EVERY part of our lives!

ACTION STEPS:

1. Listen to your thoughts and listen to what you say today. Do you need to make some adjustments with the Holy Spirit's help?
2. Let's not think thoughts that are self-serving and

detrimental to others. Instead, let's think about the good things that will produce encouraging words and great attitudes.

3. Ask Holy Spirit to help you set your mind on things above, and not just the stuff of our world, which will pass away (Colossians 3:2 NLT).

REVIEW:

1. God is a God of Peace.
2. Jesus Gave Us Peace With The Father.
3. Where God Rules Peace Is Evident.
4. Let Holy Spirit Control Your Mind.

5

HOLY SPIRIT'S TEACHINGS BRING PEACE

 *I will teach all your children, and they will enjoy great peace.*

— ISAIAH 54:13 (NLT)

O ur heavenly Father made it clear that His heart's desire was to teach every generation of His people how to live right and be at peace. As we saw in a previous chapter, Jesus came as the *Prince of Peace* and He left the gift of peace with His followers as He returned to Heaven. A key piece of information, however, was not discussed before. Namely, that Holy Spirit was integral to that peace that goes beyond our understanding. Let's look at the words of Jesus recorded in John 14:

I am telling you these things now while I am still with you. But when the Father sends the Advocate as my representative—that is, the Holy Spirit—he will teach you everything and will remind you of everything I have told you.

I am leaving you with a gift—peace of mind and heart. And the peace I give is a gift the world cannot give. So don't be troubled or afraid. Remember what I told you: I am going away, but I will come back to you again. If you really loved me, you would be happy that I am going to the Father, who is greater than I am.

— JOHN 14:25-28 (NLT)

We see here that the Holy Spirit will teach us everything. He will remind us of Jesus' words. The gift of peace will see us through the tough seasons until Jesus' return.

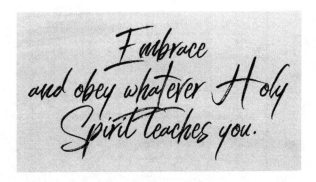

Thus, if you want to enjoy peace, you need to embrace and obey whatever the Holy Spirit teaches you. He will show you how to live and how to think as you go through life's storms.

You will live a wholesome, peaceful life that will bring joy to our Father in Heaven. You will remember that Jesus is coming soon. Your momentary troubles cannot be compared to the glory that awaits you in His eternal presence.

 For our present troubles are small and won't last very long.

Yet they produce for us a glory that vastly outweighs them and will last forever!

— 2 CORINTHIANS 4:17 (NLT)

Pick up your Bible and ask the Holy Spirit to teach you what you need to know as you represent God on this earth today.

ACTION STEPS:

1. Understand that the Lord will teach us how to get peace. He offered peace as a gift, but we have to take the necessary steps to take hold of what the Lord provided.
2. Invite Holy Spirit to instruct you in everything you do.
3. Obey your Teacher, and lean into the peace that is ours as believers in Christ Jesus. Remember, Holy Spirit's teachings bring peace!

REVIEW:

1. God is a God of Peace.
2. Jesus Gave Us Peace With The Father.
3. Where God Rules Peace Is Evident.
4. Let Holy Spirit Control Your Mind.
5. Holy Spirit's Teachings Bring Peace.

6

PEACE IS A FRUIT OF THE SPIRIT

> *But the Holy Spirit produces this kind of fruit in our lives: love, joy, peace, patience, kindness, goodness, faithfulness, gentleness, and self-control. There is no law against these things!*

— GALATIANS 5:22-23 (NLT)

Most of us have experienced both the joy and the frustration of hosting people for a week. Inevitably, the atmosphere of your home will be influenced by the types of personality such people may have. If they are enthusiastic, positive and helpful, the house will feel more energetic and hopeful. If they are cynical and cranky, the whole environment will become sluggish and subdued. After a while, no matter what you do, who they are will infect the atmosphere and mood of your home for better or worse.

In the same way, when the Holy Spirit moves into your life, His presence will produce beneficial outcomes. Paul, in our scripture above, likens these outcomes to fruit. We can expect love, joy, peace, patience kindness, goodness, faithfulness, gentleness, and self-control. That's what it's like when Holy Spirit moves in. Wow! What a blessing to have Holy Spirit in our lives! Right?

When Holy Spirit moves in, love flourishes and joy is evident to all. Subsequently, where people love each other, and pure joy is in attendance, it is just easier to be at peace. Don't you agree? Don't we all desire to be at peace with God and peace with ourselves? As a result, I think it should be much easier to be at peace with others as well.

HOLY SPIRIT'S PRESENCE PRODUCES DESIREABLE OUTCOMES.

Why? The other fruits of Holy Spirit help us do better in relating to others. Patience, kindness, goodness, faithfulness, gentleness, and self-control are integral to great relationships. Whatever we need to live in peace and harmony with God, ourselves and others, are provided by Holy Spirit who moved into our hearts!

We shared in the previous chapter that the Holy Spirit's teachings will make you peaceful. It is important to realize that He doesn't just give us instruction, but that He also empowers us. He helps us do what He teaches us to do by providing us with everything we need.

Holy Spirit is an amazing Person who fills your life with fruit. He will help you to live in peace with God, yourself and others.

ACTION STEPS:

1. Take some time right now to acknowledge the Holy Spirit.
2. Ask Holy Spirit to move in your life and to infuse all of it with His precious presence.
3. Thank Holy Spirit for the fruit, the by-product of His presence in your life. Ask Him to change the atmosphere in your heart and mind so that you can be aligned with His will today.
4. Enter your day with the knowledge that Holy Spirit will give you peace. Peace is a natural outflow of His presence and involvement in your life.

REVIEW:

1. God is a God of Peace.
2. Jesus Gave Us Peace With The Father.
3. Where God Rules Peace Is Evident.
4. Let Holy Spirit Control Your Mind.
5. Holy Spirit's Teachings Bring Peace.
6. Peace Is A Fruit Of The Spirit.

7

PEACE IS A BLESSING FROM THE LORD

> *The Lord gives his people strength. The Lord blesses them with peace.*

— PSALM 29:11 (NLT)

I f you have ever lived in an adversarial environment, you will have no problem understanding that peace, in contrast, is a huge blessing. If you have ever grown up with verbal and physical abuse, you have no problem acknowledging that peace is a highly desirable alternative. If you saw the horrors of war, you will have no difficulty understanding that peace is a precious gift.

Psalm 29:11 makes it clear that peace is one of the blessings God gives to His children. As believers, we look forward to eternity with God because we imagine Heaven to be a place saturated with God's presence and peace. Also, knowing that God desires for us to experience peace here on earth inspires me to reach for more peace in my heart, my home, and my work situation. It gives me the confidence to boldly ask God for more calm, and if there is no peace, to ask God for the strength to prevail to obtain it.

In history, great wars had been fought to secure peace between neighboring clans and countries. Peace doesn't come without sacrifice. Sometimes we have to engage the enemy to reclaim our inheritance from the Lord.

For example, God promised the Israelites the blessings and provision of the *Promised Land*. Regardless of the promise, they still had to cross over the Jordan and contend for it with the occupying nations. There is often a fierce opposition to your peace mission. You must be bold, strong, and courageous to get the peace that is rightfully yours.

Jesus characterized the enemy as a thief, a murderer, and

destroyer[1]. Know that the enemy, your adversary, tries to steal your blessing of peace every day. Peace is such a precious blessing from the Lord that our enemy will do anything to rob us of its benefits. He would rather have us miserable, fighting and complaining than being in a blissful state of serenity, praising the Lord!

Most likely, you can remember days filled with peace, only to have that peace shattered by an unexpected development. You are not alone. We all have had to pick up the broken pieces to rebuild and restore God's peace in our lives. Make a decision today that you are going to receive God's peace. Then, boldly protect His peace as if your life depends upon it!

ACTION STEPS:

1. Know that God blesses His children with peace.
2. If you don't have any peace, ask the Lord for strength so you can fight to get your peace back from your enemy, the devil.
3. When you have prevailed in prayer and have had your peace restored to you, please be vigilant not to lose it along the way.
4. Don't allow anybody to pickpocket your peace!
5. Remember, peace is God's blessing to His children.
6. Look for and recognize the benefits of God's peace in your family, at work, at church, and in the community.
7. Be grateful for God's peace blessing!

REVIEW:

1. God is a God of Peace.
2. Jesus Gave Us Peace With The Father.
3. Where God Rules Peace Is Evident.
4. Let Holy Spirit Control Your Mind.
5. Holy Spirit's Teachings Bring Peace.
6. Peace Is A Fruit Of The Spirit.
7. Peace Is A Blessing From The Lord.

---

1. See John 10:10.

8

FIX YOUR THOUGHTS ON GOD AND OBTAIN PEACE

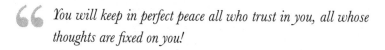 *You will keep in perfect peace all who trust in you, all whose thoughts are fixed on you!*

— ISAIAH 26:3 (NLT)

The prophet Isaiah was inspired by the Holy Spirit to pen this encouragement to God's people in the midst of tough times. He was letting them know that if they trust in the Lord and if they can fix their thoughts on Him they will be sustained in perfect peace.

Our times may not be as filled with danger as it was for this ancient audience, but we have our share of modern troubles to contend with. We too stumble headlong under the weights of responsibilities and modern stress. Those ancient words ring true in the ears of believers everywhere today: Trust God, think about His benefits, and you will be at peace!

An ancient king, renowned for his wisdom, wrote this for our consideration:

> *Trust in the Lord with all your heart; do not depend on your own understanding. Seek his will in all you do, and he will show you which path to take.*

> — PROVERBS 3:5-6 (NLT)

Often our fears and anxieties occur because we are not sure which way to go. We do not know what to say. However, if we trust the Lord, He will show us what is right. We must focus on God and obey His will in everything we do.

I have read that when there is a hurricane on the surface of the ocean, surprisingly, a few feet down, it is calm. In the same way, it may seem like everything in our lives is negatively impacted by powerful forces beyond our control. However, deep within, we can be cool, calm and collected. We know that in all things God is working for our good[1].

There is an excellent peace in knowing that our Heavenly Father knows best. As we focus our minds on Him, He will be faithful to lead us like a good shepherd. Paul wrote his audience to always think about the right stuff, regardless of what the world threw at them:

> *And now, dear brothers and sisters, one final thing. Fix your thoughts on what is true, and honorable, and right, and pure, and lovely, and admirable. Think about things that are excellent and worthy of praise. Keep putting into practice all you learned and received from me—everything you heard from me and saw me doing. Then the God of peace will be with you.*
>
> — PHILIPPIANS 4:8-9 (NLT)

Who is true, honorable, right, pure, lovely and admirable? Who does things that are excellent and worthy of praise? Our God! Our amazing God has all of those wonderful attributes!

Paul also wrote about them doing what is right, what is righteous, and what pleases the Lord. He wanted his readers to experience the God of peace in their lives! See, if you will trust the Lord, and fix your thoughts on the good God you serve, He will help you to live right and do right. He will empower you to imitate Him. He will be the peace that sustains you.

ACTION STEPS:

1. Who do you trust?
2. Who don't you trust?
3. Do you *really* trust the Lord?
4. Do you trust Him *beyond* your understanding?
5. Are you focusing your thoughts and meditations on who God is and what He is about?
6. Are you doing what is good and right?
7. Are you expecting the peace God and the God of Peace to fill your day?
8. Good. Keep it up! Keep your peace!

REVIEW:

1. God is a God of Peace.
2. Jesus Gave Us Peace With The Father.
3. Where God Rules Peace Is Evident.
4. Let Holy Spirit Control Your Mind.
5. Holy Spirit's Teachings Bring Peace.
6. Peace Is A Fruit Of The Spirit.
7. Peace Is A Blessing From The Lord.
8. Fix Your Thoughts On God And Obtain Peace.

---

1. See Romans 8:28.

9

LET PEACE RULE YOUR HEART

> *Since God chose you to be the holy people he loves, you must clothe yourselves with tenderhearted mercy, kindness, humility, gentleness, and patience. Make allowance for each other's faults, and forgive anyone who offends you. Remember, the Lord forgave you, so you must forgive others. Above all, clothe yourselves with love, which binds us all together in perfect harmony. And let the peace that comes from Christ rule in your hearts. For as members of one body you are called to live in peace. And always be thankful.*

— COLOSSIANS 3:12-15 (NLT)

When you read this portion of scripture, it can be difficult to imagine peace ruling and having *dominion* in our hearts. Our world is just too upsetting, we may think. The writer made it clear here that we must *choose* to put on six distinctive attitudes: mercy, kindness, humility, gentleness, patience, and forgiveness. Then, we are to tie them together with love.

Wow! I think that extending forgiveness will be especially hard if you don't *choose* to love those who have offended you. I believe that it is impossible to find peace with God and others until we learn to let go of offenses. That's why *The Believer's Prayer*, also known as *The Lord's Prayer,* contains the words, *"Forgive us our debts as we forgive our debtors.*[1]*"*

Forgiveness is a golden key to peace in our hearts. We have been forgiven, and we, likewise, should forgive as we have been forgiven. Many, many people live in torment and do not know peace because they refuse to let go and let God fix others.

If you refuse to forgive someone right now, please remember that Jesus forgave you a lifetime of sins. Surely you can forgive someone for their trespasses against you. Please, do it now!

Ask Holy Spirit to help you. Let the Lord help them with their mistakes today. You have enough of your own to deal with on a given day. You cannot even fix yourself. Stop trying to fix others as if they are broken. Forgive and move on. You will travel a lot lighter without all that baggage from the past. You will live lighter, sleep better and laugh more, trust me.

Then, only then, the peace that Christ gives can have dominion of our heart. Then he continues with our first portion of scripture:

> *And let the peace that comes from Christ rule in your hearts. For as members of one body you are called to live in peace. And always be thankful.*

— COLOSSIANS 3:12-15 (NLT)

Notice, he wrote, *always* be thankful. After we choose to cooperate with God's plan, peace will rule in our hearts. Gratitude will be the expected by-product. If you have a hard time to be grateful, go through the preceding steps to see what is missing. Make the necessary adjustments.

So, let's do that today. Let's put on those six attitudes. Let's tie them together with love. Finally, let peace rule in your heart. Oh yes, don't forget to be thankful!

ACTION STEPS:

1. As you face the rest of the day, put on mercy. Don't try to take revenge. Don't be judge, jury, and executioner.
2. Kindness is the opposite of meanness. Choose kindness.
3. Be humble. Pride comes before a fall.
4. Be gentle. You don't know what others are battling.

5. Be patient. Enough said.

6. Forgive others, because God forgave you first.

7. Read I Corinthians 13's definition of love. Do that.

8. Let peace rule. From our scripture, we see that peace is a choice and an outcome resulting from the right decisions.

9. When you feel the peace welling up in your heart, don't forget to be thankful. God is good.

REVIEW:

1. God is a God of Peace.

2. Jesus Gave Us Peace With The Father.

3. Where God Rules Peace Is Evident.

4. Let Holy Spirit Control Your Mind.

5. Holy Spirit's Teachings Bring Peace.

6. Peace Is A Fruit Of The Spirit.

7. Peace Is A Blessing From The Lord.

8. Fix Your Thoughts On God And Obtain Peace.

9. Let Peace Rule Your Heart.

---

1. See Matthew 6:9-13 and Luke 11:2-4.

10

LOVE PEACE

> *Look at those who are honest and good, for a wonderful future awaits those who love peace.*

> — PSALM 37:37 (NLT)

It is interesting how much attention we give to people who love to fight, brawl, argue, split hairs and cause division in our modern culture. Our news channels have discussion panels with red-faced pundits showing disrespect towards anyone who does not share their point of view. It's angry, toxic and stress-inducing to anyone who views it. I cannot bear to watch any of it anymore, whether it is on television or social media. Hatred has bled into the fabric of our culture. Rancor is spilling into our interactions with our fellow-citizens and family members.

The psalmist encourages us to take a time-out from such an adversarial life. We should search for a godly alternative. He admonishes us to turn our eyes away from the purveyors of divisiveness. Instead, we should look at those who are honest and kind. I like the *Amplified Bible's* translation of our scripture:

> *Mark the blameless man (who is spiritually complete), and behold the upright (who walks in moral integrity); There is a (good) future for the man of peace (because a life of honor blesses one's descendants).*

— PSALM 37:37 (AMP)

We can celebrate good and honest people over others who lie and do anything they can to get negative attention. We can turn away from those who define themselves by their defiance of God and His Word. Why do we award the ungodly with our attention and our entertainment dollars? Is it any wonder that we are so unhappy as a culture? Hopelessness and despair reign. We feel overwhelmed because we think we will never quite gain enough or be enough.

Isn't it time for us to celebrate the pure beauty of honesty and integrity? Isn't it time to once again love peace more than conflict? Conflict and war may seem more interesting at first, but the human heart will ultimately cry out for peace.

There is a desire for a cessation of the endless hostility that defines our fallen world. We do not look for peace only in the present, but also in the future, for the benefit of subsequent generations.

I like to watch a show on *PBS* called **Who Do You Think You Are?** Celebrity actors receive help from genealogy experts to trace the lives of their ancestors. You see the actors in joyful tears when they find out that their ancestors did something particularly noble or charitable. You also see actors perplexed and grieved when they find out that an ancestor chose an evil path to walk in the past. In this show, I saw first-hand how a life of honor will bless one's descendants, just like the psalmist points out in our scripture.

When we love peace and live honest and ethical lives, our descendants will one day hear our stories and be blessed. They will stand on our shoulders and do even better than we have done with God's help in their generation. For your sake and the sake of generations to come, love God and love peace!

ACTION STEPS:

1. Today, let's use our energy and time to fill our lives with honesty and goodness. Celebrate people who

are making positive contributions. Don't spend your time pointing out how dysfunctional others are.

2. Commit to refrain from reading or adding to the angry conversations going on in social media channels. It's hard to love peace and add fuel to fires of resentment at the same time.

3. Let's commit to love peace more than conflict and division.

REVIEW:

1. God is a God of Peace.
2. Jesus Gave Us Peace With The Father.
3. Where God Rules Peace Is Evident.
4. Let Holy Spirit Control Your Mind.
5. Holy Spirit's Teachings Bring Peace.
6. Peace Is A Fruit Of The Spirit.
7. Peace Is A Blessing From The Lord.
8. Fix Your Thoughts On God And Obtain Peace.
9. Let Peace Rule Your Heart.
10. Love Peace.

11

JESUS' WORDS BRING PEACE

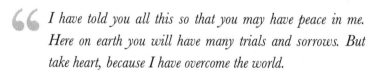 *I have told you all this so that you may have peace in me. Here on earth you will have many trials and sorrows. But take heart, because I have overcome the world.*

— JOHN 16:33 (NLT)

Jesus was telling His disciples that the default setting in a fallen world is, *"many trials and sorrows."* I wanted to hear Jesus tell them that after His resurrection all trials and sorrows will be over. I wanted to hear that, since the devil was defeated, I can relax and enjoy a smooth, trouble-free ride through this world until I reach Heaven.

However, Jesus told them that they could take heart because He had overcome the world. The world used to be undefeated, but Jesus came and broke that perfect record. In Him, we can overcome the world as well. With Him indwelling us by Holy Spirit, we can be more than conquerors. We have the benefit of engaging the enemy with the same holy power that defeated him on resurrection day. Paul did a beautiful summary of what Jesus helped us obtain:

> *What then shall we say to these things? If God is for us, who can be against us? He who did not spare His own Son, but delivered Him up for us all, how shall He not with Him also freely give us all things? Who shall bring a charge against God's elect? It is God who justifies. Who is he who condemns? It is Christ who died, and furthermore is also risen, who is even at the right hand of God, who also makes intercession for us. Who shall separate us from the love of Christ? Shall tribulation, or distress, or persecution, or famine, or nakedness, or peril, or sword? As it is written: 'For Your sake we are killed all day long; We are accounted as sheep for the slaughter.' Yet in all these things we are more than conquerors through Him who loved us. For I am persuaded that neither death nor life, nor angels nor principalities nor powers, nor things present nor things to come, nor height nor depth, nor any other created thing, shall be able to separate us from the love of God which is in Christ Jesus our Lord.*

> — ROMANS 8:31-39 (NKJV)

That's why we can have peace in Jesus. We should not allow our hearts to be troubled. We should draw courage from the fact that we now fight side-by-side with the Lord. This is apparent when you read the last verses of the *Gospel of Mark*:

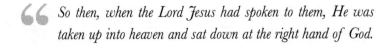

> *So then, when the Lord Jesus had spoken to them, He was taken up into heaven and sat down at the right hand of God.*

And they went out and preached everywhere, while the Lord was working with them and confirming the word by the signs that followed.

— MARK 16:19-20 (AMP)

The Lord was with them, fighting alongside His disciples as they pushed back the darkness with the preaching of the Good News and by praying for the sick and oppressed. Yes, they still had troubles and trials, but they were encouraged because the Lord was helping them win! As they obeyed His instructions and fulfilled their calling, their hearts were filled with peace, and they courageously faced every difficulty.

hear THE WORDS OF JESUS AND experience peace.

I pray that you will hear the words of Jesus. I pray that you will allow His words to bring you peace as you face your trials and troubles. Remember, be at peace, because you are not alone. Don't fear any harm coming your way.

But all who listen to me will live in peace, untroubled by fear of harm.

— PROVERBS 1:33 (NLT)

ACTION STEPS:

1. Remember that you are not alone in this world of many troubles. The Lord is a prayer away. Talk to Him about your fears and challenges.
2. Jesus is still the undefeated champion of the world. He is fighting for you and with you to defeat the enemy in your situation.
3. Tell others the *Good News* you have received about Jesus. Expect some people to get healed, saved and delivered. Jesus is ready to step in and help you do it.
4. Study the words of the Lord and allow Holy Spirit to bring them to remembrance. Our last scripture promises that if you do that, you will live in peace, untroubled by fear of harm.

REVIEW:

1. God is a God of Peace.
2. Jesus Gave Us Peace With The Father.
3. Where God Rules Peace Is Evident.
4. Let Holy Spirit Control Your Mind.

5. Holy Spirit's Teachings Bring Peace.
6. Peace Is A Fruit Of The Spirit.
7. Peace Is A Blessing From The Lord.
8. Fix Your Thoughts On God And Obtain Peace.
9. Let Peace Rule Your Heart.
10. Love Peace.
11. Jesus' Words Bring Peace.

12

PEACE OF MIND AND HEART

> *I am leaving you with a gift—peace of mind and heart. And the peace I give is a gift the world cannot give. So don't be troubled or afraid.*

— JOHN 14:27 (NLT)

J esus spoke these words to His disciples right before His crucifixion. He knew that shortly after He talked to them, they will be running for their lives, trying to avoid capture by the Jewish authorities. He was reassuring them that His peace could sustain them through the fiercest opposition and trails. Later, those words carried them forward when they had to face many challenges and persecution.

Before this they were all with Jesus on that stormy night at sea, when they all feared for their lives:

> *As evening came, Jesus said to his disciples, 'Let's cross to*

the other side of the lake.' So they took Jesus in the boat and started out, leaving the crowds behind (although other boats followed). But soon a fierce storm came up. High waves were breaking into the boat, and it began to fill with water. Jesus was sleeping at the back of the boat with his head on a cushion. The disciples woke him up, shouting, 'Teacher, don't you care that we're going to drown?' When Jesus woke up, he rebuked the wind and said to the waves, 'Silence! Be still!' Suddenly the wind stopped, and there was a great calm. Then he asked them, 'Why are you afraid? Do you still have no faith?' The disciples were absolutely terrified. 'Who is this man?' they asked each other. 'Even the wind and waves obey him!'

— MARK 4:35-41 (NLT)

Jesus was asleep, undisturbed by the howling wind and the thunderous clouds of rain. They awoke him, clamoring for His attention, incredulous that He did not care about their pending demise. He just addressed the wind and calmed the waves. When everything calmed down, He rebuked them for their lack of faith. They were astonished at His authority over the elements and His calm response to what was a life-threatening situation.

Jesus, by His example, was teaching them how to be at peace in a storm. Later, when He told them about His gift of peace to them, He encouraged them not to be troubled or afraid. I don't know if you are facing a storm that has the adrenaline surging through your system as fear is gripping your heart. I don't know what your storm sounds like or feels like, but I do know what the

Lord's words are to you right now. Let's reread His words and make them personal, to you specifically:

> *I am leaving you with a gift—peace of mind and heart. And the peace I give is a gift the world cannot give. So don't be troubled or afraid.*

—JOHN 14:27 (NLT)

"I'm Still Standing." Young woman buffeted by powerful wind is able to stand in God's strength. (Colored pens on paper by Iann Schonken, 2016)

We cannot keep the storms of life from filling our boats with water, but we can stop them from filling us with fear. If Jesus is in your boat, talk to Him about your storm. Then, talk to your storm about Jesus! Just like in that story from the Gospels, you and Jesus are going over to *the other side*. He will never leave you nor forsake you. Let Jesus be the Prince of Peace in your mind and heart, and then, tell your storm that Jesus is Lord!

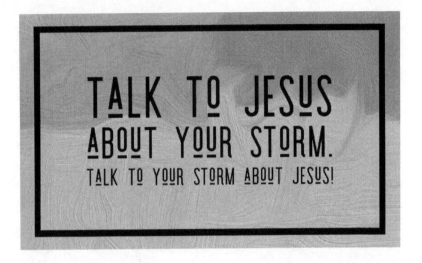

ACTION STEPS:

1. Believe Jesus and receive your gift of peace. If I tell you that I left you a bonus check on the mantle in the living room, it is up to you to go and pick it up, open it, and receive it. How you use it is your prerogative. Say to yourself, *"I have received my gift of peace from Jesus, and nobody is going to rob me of my peace today!"*

2. Stop looking for your peace in the world. The world is unable to give you peace because all it can offer is turmoil and pain. Even nature can be brutal if you try to find peace there. Think about it: You can sit on

a rock enjoying the scenery and get a snake bite! Get
your peace from God. It's His gift to you today.

3. Make a decision that you are not going to react
fearfully to anything that happens in your life.
Respond to everything by having great faith in God!

REVIEW:

1. God is a God of Peace.
2. Jesus Gave Us Peace With The Father.
3. Where God Rules Peace Is Evident.
4. Let Holy Spirit Control Your Mind.
5. Holy Spirit's Teachings Bring Peace.
6. Peace Is A Fruit Of The Spirit.
7. Peace Is A Blessing From The Lord.
8. Fix Your Thoughts On God And Obtain Peace.
9. Let Peace Rule Your Heart.
10. Love Peace.
11. Jesus' Words Bring Peace.
12. Peace of Mind and Heart.

13

TRUSTING GOD LEADS TO PEACEFUL SLEEP

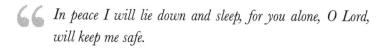 *In peace I will lie down and sleep, for you alone, O Lord, will keep me safe.*

— PSALM 4:8 (NLT)

According to an article at *Harvard Medical School*'s web site, we spend about a third of our lives asleep[1]. The sad reality is, tens of millions of Americans do not get the sleep their bodies need. Nearly 20% of American adults report using some kind of sleep medication. Some have turned to alcohol for relief, and others have seemingly tried everything without relief[2]. Can you relate to that?

As for myself, I have spent my share of sleepless nights, rolling over and over in my bed for hours. I couldn't stop mulling over some vexing problem with a co-worker. Maybe I wake up in the middle of the night, grab a glass of water and my brain kicks in. I cannot get any more sleep no matter how hard I try. I start to imagine everything that can go wrong in my situation. I have conversations in my head with people who are blissfully asleep, unaware of my sleepless suffering! The next day I feel weak. I go around like a zombie with black rings under my bloodshot eyes as I down cups of coffee to stay awake.

We should all agree that it is futility! It is futile to lose precious sleep and my health because I cannot let go of what I cannot change.

> *Fatigue distorts reality and magnifies offenses and disappointments.*
>
> — MIKE MURDOCK

The psalmist, who had his share of troubles and enemies, realized that to meditate on anything other than God's all-sufficient provision is ridiculous! To worry about tomorrow's problems only robs us of our desperately needed rest tonight. I have also found that most of the things I fearfully anticipated never showed up the next day. I just foolishly chose to get stuck in a *worst-case scenario simulation loop*! As a result, I became all anxious and fretful. I forgot that the Lord cares for me and that He was waiting for me ....

> *Cast all your anxiety on him because he cares for you.*
>
> — 1 PETER 5:7 (NIV)

I was holding on to what I needed to give to God. Elsewhere, the psalmist adds another nugget of wisdom for us to consider:

Unless the Lord builds the house, they labor in vain who build it; unless the Lord guards the city, the watchman keeps awake in vain. It is vain for you to rise early, to retire late, to eat the bread of anxious labors— for He gives blessings to His beloved even in his sleep.

— PSALM 127:1-2 (AMP)

What? You mean I stayed up and worried about things I couldn't change while God was already working to solve my problems? You say I could have prayed, and I could have had a good night's rest?! Yup! Pretty much.

Why don't you try this tonight when you go to bed? Tell God that you trust Him with your troubles. Thank Him that He promised to take care of some things while you sleep. Then close your eyes and sleep like a baby. Stop being so anxious. The Lord's got this! Just trust Him.

ACTION STEPS:

1. What concerns you?
2. Tell God you trust Him to help you.
3. Thank Him for a good night's rest. Your body needs it.
4. Let it go. Let God do what God does. You do what you need to do: Rest.

REVIEW:

1. God is a God of Peace.
2. Jesus Gave Us Peace With The Father.
3. Where God Rules Peace Is Evident.
4. Let Holy Spirit Control Your Mind.
5. Holy Spirit's Teachings Bring Peace.
6. Peace Is A Fruit Of The Spirit.
7. Peace Is A Blessing From The Lord.
8. Fix Your Thoughts On God And Obtain Peace.
9. Let Peace Rule Your Heart.
10. Love Peace.
11. Jesus' Words Bring Peace.
12. Peace of Mind and Heart.
13. Trusting God Leads To Peaceful Sleep.

---

1. See Suzanne Bertisch, MD, MPH, "*No More Counting Sheep: Proven Behaviors to Help You Sleep.*" Harvard Health Publishing, November 5, 2018, www.health.harvard.edu/blog/no-more-counting-sheep-proven-behaviors-to-help-you-sleep-2018110515313

2. *Ibid.*

14

THERE IS NO PEACE FOR THE WICKED

 'But there is no peace for the wicked,' says the Lord.

— ISAIAH 48:22 (NLT)

W e have looked for several chapters at how God blesses His people with peace. I think that when people have served the Lord for a long time, they tend to forget just how bad it is for people who don't live in a realm of peace. They almost get bored with peace, and they are tempted to go and do some *exciting* things like the people in the world do. We will do well to remember what the world looks like without peace. Isaiah the prophet paints a vivid picture of the wretched lives of the wicked in his writings:

 It's your sins that have cut you off from God. Because of your sins, he has turned away and will not listen anymore. Your hands are the hands of murderers, and your fingers are filthy with sin. Your lips are full of lies, and your mouth

spews corruption. No one cares about being fair and honest. The people's lawsuits are based on lies. They conceive evil deeds and then give birth to sin. They hatch deadly snakes and weave spiders' webs. Whoever eats their eggs will die; whoever cracks them will hatch a viper. Their webs can't be made into clothing, and nothing they do is productive. All their activity is filled with sin, and violence is their trademark. Their feet run to do evil, and they rush to commit murder. They think only about sinning. Misery and destruction always follow them. They don't know where to find peace or what it means to be just and good. They have mapped out crooked roads, and no one who follows them knows a moment's peace.

— ISAIAH 9:2-8 (NLT)

I don't know about you, but I want to run as far as I can from that kind of life. Whatever *excitement* exists there is short-lived and ultimately condemned to painful failure! It clearly states that they don't know where to find peace or what it means to be good. Even those that hang out with them are doomed to a peace-less life!

Ezekiel, another Old Testament prophet, paints a picture of what happens to people who abandon their place of peace with God:

> *Terror and trembling will overcome my people. They will look for peace but not find it.*
>
> — EZEKIEL 7:25 (NLT)

Both these scriptures speak of God's people abandoning their place of being blessed by God. They try out the excitements and enticements of the world. These scriptures make it clear that to leave God is to leave peace behind. God does not lie. There is no peace for the wicked.

ACTION STEPS:

1. Have you become a little bored with the Christian life of being honest and kind? Are you sometimes tempted with the kind of life that many are living in the world? Do you sometimes wonder if it will not be more fun to live like some of the celebrities on

television who seem to do whatever they want and still live a great life?

2. Remind yourself that there is no peace for the wicked apart from God. Gold turns into sand when you don't have peace in your life.

3. Enjoy the peace God gives. Be grateful for the blessings of the Lord that add no sorrow. Don't be tempted by what the wicked sells. Go and read Psalm 37. It will help you understand just how good you have it with the Lord.

REVIEW:

1. God is a God of Peace.
2. Jesus Gave Us Peace With The Father.
3. Where God Rules Peace Is Evident.
4. Let Holy Spirit Control Your Mind.
5. Holy Spirit's Teachings Bring Peace.
6. Peace Is A Fruit Of The Spirit.
7. Peace Is A Blessing From The Lord.
8. Fix Your Thoughts On God And Obtain Peace.
9. Let Peace Rule Your Heart.
10. Love Peace.
11. Jesus' Words Bring Peace.
12. Peace of Mind and Heart.
13. Trusting God Leads To Peaceful Sleep.
14. There Is No Peace For The Wicked.

15

DOING GOOD RESULTS IN PEACE

> *But there will be glory and honor and peace from God for all who do good—for the Jew first and also for the Gentile.*

— ROMANS 2:10 (NLT)

To do good, to live right, and to go *with* God as opposed to going *against* God, bring about peaceful outcomes. Our scripture confirms that God will shine His glory and honor on such people. We saw in the previous chapter what the wicked, disobedient person's life looks like. It is clear that going against the grain of what God desires results in painful splinters. In contrast, doing God's will creates a smooth pathway towards ultimate blessings and honor.

The twenty-third Psalm is David's song about the Lord being his Shepherd. Let's look at it with today's lesson in mind:

> *The Lord is my shepherd; I have all that I need. He lets me rest in green meadows; he leads me beside peaceful streams.*

He renews my strength. He guides me along right paths, bringing honor to his name. Even when I walk through the darkest valley, I will not be afraid, for you are close beside me. Your rod and your staff protect and comfort me. You prepare a feast for me in the presence of my enemies. You honor me by anointing my head with oil. My cup overflows with blessings. Surely your goodness and unfailing love will pursue me all the days of my life, and I will live in the house of the Lord forever.

— PSALM 23 (NLT)

PEACE IS A REWARD FOR LIVING RIGHT IN A WORLD GONE WRONG.

How do the sheep get to peaceful streams? By following the Shepherd. The only way to follow the Shepherd is to obey the Shepherd and to stay with Him. The Shepherd leads the sheep through some dangerous places and past some formidable enemies. The Shepherd also provides guidance, safety, and oversight of what happens next. The Shepherd leads His sheep all the way, never leaving or forsaking them.

They have only one thing they *must* do: They must follow and obey the Shepherd. When you do your best to follow God by doing His will, it will ultimately result in your life being distinguished by glory, honor, and peace. Today, we must tell ourselves that peace is not just a person, a gift, or a goal. Peace is a reward for living right in a world gone wrong. It's a fruit, an outcome of maturing as a child of God.

Follow the Lord, obey His Word, and you will experience peace that is beyond your understanding.

ACTION STEPS:

1. Follow the Good Shepherd. Obey His Word.
2. Even when in a dangerous place, know that your obedience to God will bring glory and honor to God.
3. Expect God to anoint your head with oil. Expect your cup of joy to overflow.
4. Remember, goodness and mercy shall follow you all the days of your life, and you will dwell in the house of the Lord forever!
5. Expect God's peace to be around you and within your heart. He loves you very much, and He desires to bless you with glory, honor, and peace.

REVIEW:

1. God is a God of Peace.
2. Jesus Gave Us Peace With The Father.
3. Where God Rules Peace Is Evident.

4. Let Holy Spirit Control Your Mind.

5. Holy Spirit's Teachings Bring Peace.

6. Peace Is A Fruit Of The Spirit.

7. Peace Is A Blessing From The Lord.

8. Fix Your Thoughts On God And Obtain Peace.

9. Let Peace Rule Your Heart.

10. Love Peace.

11. Jesus' Words Bring Peace.

12. Peace of Mind and Heart.

13. Trusting God Leads To Peaceful Sleep.

14. There Is No Peace For The Wicked.

15. Doing Good Results In Peace.

16

PLAN FOR PEACE AND EXPERIENCE JOY

> *Deceit fills hearts that are plotting evil; joy fills hearts that are planning peace!*

— PROVERBS 12:20 (NLT)

> *"A goal without a plan is just a wish."*

— ANTOINE DE SAINT-EXUPÉRY

A nyone can wish for more peace in their lives, but peace requires more than just a desire. To taste the delightful sweetness of peace in your day will require some intentionality on your part. Many are the obstacles and challenges awaiting you, and the evil one plans diligently to bring you down. Your destruction is his desire, and you will have to devise a strategy to obtain and maintain your peace.

It is a great relief to know that God has a plan for us. He is not leaving it all to randomness:

> *For I know the thoughts that I think toward you, says the Lord, thoughts of peace and not of evil, to give you a future and a hope.*

> — JEREMIAH 29:11 (NKJV)

Jesus said that He came to bring us an abundant life. That was Jesus' plan for us, but He introduced His plan with a warning: Our enemy comes to kill, steal and destroy (see John 10:10). Wow! A good plan and an evil enemy? What are we to do then?

I'd say that we need to stay close to the Lord throughout the day! We need to listen to Holy Spirit as He directs us in different situations. We need to avoid events that may stir up clouds of fear, doubt, and unbelief in our hearts. We may have to side-step people that threaten the peace of the Lord in our moments. Some of them are unavoidable, but we can choose our responses to such people. We may need to turn off those talk radio shows, newscasts or podcasts that stir negative emotions in us. We cannot leave this to chance; we must have a plan!

We must plan to avoid social media channels and television shows that depress rather than uplift us. I believe each of us can discern such people, places, and events that have left us without peace in the past. I also think that with careful planning and strategic navigation throughout the day, we can seek out people and places that feed our faith.

There is a joy that comes from planning for the peace you desire in your life. Today, make up your mind that nobody is going to offend you into a state of anger and unforgiveness. Plan your day so you can live in peace. Yes, there will be opposition, but you can plan to succeed in your mission. Remember, our scripture today tells us that joy fills hearts that are planning peace!

What is your plan for joy and peace today? I believe that the Lord will bless you with wisdom and peace from above:

> *But the wisdom from above is first of all pure. It is also peace loving, gentle at all times, and willing to yield to others. It is full of mercy and the fruit of good deeds. It shows no favoritism and is always sincere. And those who are peacemakers will plant seeds of peace and reap a harvest of righteousness.*

> — JAMES 3:17-18 (NLT)

Plan your day so you can live in peace.

ACTION STEPS:

1. What is your peace plan for today? Don't have one? Grab a pen and paper. Start writing down a few things you can do to have a more peaceful day.
2. What steals your peace? Who pickpockets your peace? Which shows and social media channels take your peace? How can you avoid or minimize such negative influences and the anxiety they bring into your life?
3. Ask the Holy Spirit to help you discern how you can strategically avoid things that steal your peace. Ask Him how to go about cultivating peace and joy in your life.

REVIEW:

1. God is a God of Peace.
2. Jesus Gave Us Peace With The Father.
3. Where God Rules Peace Is Evident.
4. Let Holy Spirit Control Your Mind.
5. Holy Spirit's Teachings Bring Peace.
6. Peace Is A Fruit Of The Spirit.
7. Peace Is A Blessing From The Lord.
8. Fix Your Thoughts On God And Obtain Peace.
9. Let Peace Rule Your Heart.
10. Love Peace.
11. Jesus' Words Bring Peace.

12. Peace of Mind and Heart.
13. Trusting God Leads To Peaceful Sleep.
14. There Is No Peace For The Wicked.
15. Doing Good Results In Peace.
16. Plan For Peace And Experience Joy.

PLEASE GOD AND EXPERIENCE PEACE WITH YOUR ENEMIES

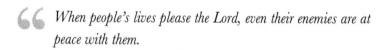 *When people's lives please the Lord, even their enemies are at peace with them.*

— PROVERBS 16:7 (NLT)

W e are all unique and different from others in many ways. Those differences are what make us attractive to some and irritating to others. It is challenging not to rub somebody the wrong way as you go through life. In spite of our best efforts, people can choose to become our enemies. They oppose us because our differences are not compatible with their unique perspectives or assignments in life.

The realities of difference and the inevitability of conflict create vexing challenges as we look for peace with others. It is very hard to be at peace with yourself when someone is not at peace with you.

Our scripture today brings a gift of hope to us. It promises that our enemies can be brought into a place of peace with us. I believe that, with the Lord's help, we can obtain favor even with our enemies. The wise writer made it clear that the first step towards a peace with enemies is to live a life that pleases the Lord.

> it is hard to be at peace with yourself when someone isn't at peace with you.

Elsewhere, a psalmist sings:

> *Take delight in the Lord, and he will give you your heart's desires.*
>
> — PSALM 37:4 (NLT)

How do we delight in and please the Lord? We please and satisfy the Lord by studying the Bible every day, learning the principles of living like Him:

> *Oh, the joys of those who do not follow the advice of the*

wicked, or stand around with sinners, or join in with mockers. But they delight in the law of the Lord, meditating on it day and night. They are like trees planted along the riverbank, bearing fruit each season. Their leaves never wither, and they prosper in all they do. But not the wicked! They are like worthless chaff, scattered by the wind. They will be condemned at the time of judgment. Sinners will have no place among the godly. For the Lord watches over the path of the godly, but the path of the wicked leads to destruction.

— PSALM 1 (NLT)

Do you see the positive results of studying God's will and living accordingly? You will prosper in everything you do! More than that, even if someone feels jealous of the blessings of God in your life, God will cause them to change their minds about you:

When the LORD takes pleasure in anyone's way, he causes their enemies to make peace with them.

— PROVERBS 16:7 (NIV)

This translation sounds a little different from our original text. It suggests that God *causes* the adversarial person to look with favor on you because of God's intervention. You may think it impossible to change the hearts of your adversaries, but never underestimate God's ability to shape human opinions about you! God can even turn a king's heart towards you if He wills:

> *The king's heart is like channels of water in the hand of the Lord; He turns it wherever He wishes.*
>
> — PROVERBS 21:1 (NASB)

When you please God, you can experience peace with your enemies! Focus on pleasing God, and it may very well result in a surprising harmony with your new friends... your previous enemies.

ACTION STEPS:

1. Has your uniqueness caused a rift between you and others? Have the blessings of God stirred up jealousy and strife? If so, know that you are not alone. However, remember that the Lord can help you with your enemies.

2. Jesus calls us to love and pray for our enemies (Matthew 5:44). If you study God's will, you will bump into this scripture, and you will be overwhelmed by the difficulty of doing what it requires. However, choose to delight yourself in the Lord and endeavor to forgive and forget. Pray for your adversaries and bless them. You'll be glad you did!

3. Expect the Lord to give you favor with your enemies. Expect peace in spite of what divides you. Remember, it is our differences that create diversity

and beauty around us. Celebrate the differences and learn from the uniqueness God created in each one of us. Delight yourself in the Lord, and expect favor from others.

REVIEW:

1. God is a God of Peace.
2. Jesus Gave Us Peace With The Father.
3. Where God Rules Peace Is Evident.
4. Let Holy Spirit Control Your Mind.
5. Holy Spirit's Teachings Bring Peace.
6. Peace Is A Fruit Of The Spirit.
7. Peace Is A Blessing From The Lord.
8. Fix Your Thoughts On God And Obtain Peace.
9. Let Peace Rule Your Heart.
10. Love Peace.
11. Jesus' Words Bring Peace.
12. Peace of Mind and Heart.
13. Trusting God Leads To Peaceful Sleep.
14. There Is No Peace For The Wicked.
15. Doing Good Results In Peace.
16. Plan For Peace And Experience Joy.
17. Please God And Experience Peace With Your Enemies.

GOD'S CHILDREN ARE PEACEMAKERS

66 *God blesses those who work for peace, for they will be called the children of God.*

— MATTHEW 5:9 (NLT)

I n the *Sermon on the Mount,* Jesus listed all the people who are blessed by God. Those who *work for peace* are in that elite group of highly-favored people. I prefer the older translations that call them *peacemakers.* It captures the sense of *a process of making,* as opposed to merely a state of *being.*

Know this: Peace is *made.* While peace shows up when God shows up, people still have to labor diligently to align themselves with the will of the Lord. They have to work hard to share that sense of serenity with everyone else in a situation.

Peace has to be negotiated in all human cultures. Peace talks usually entail a lot of back-and-forth communication to ensure that everyone is on the same page and of the same mind. Peacemakers are known for being fully engaged in this peace-making process and are opposed to fueling division and conflict.

A great example of a peacemaker is found in the Old Testament of the Bible. The young man David, before he was crowned king, had been living near a landlord named Nabal. It was time for the shearing of sheep and David requested some food and provisions for the 600 or so men who accompanied him[1]. He felt that his men had provided security to Nabal's herdsmen and that it was not an unreasonable request. Nabal rudely rebuffed David, and David quickly mustered 400 of his men into an army to annihilate Nabal for his insulting response.

Meanwhile, Abigail, Nabal's wife, heard about what happened and quickly gathered a peace offering of food and wine. She rushed to meet David and his men as they prepared for their assault on Nabal's home. She spoke eloquently, beseeching David to relent and to receive her gift as compensation for her husband's foolish response. David relaxed, and Abigail returned home with the tragedy averted.

She wisely waited for her husband to be sober before she told him about what had happened. He was filled with dread when he realized the potential consequences of his actions. The Bible states that he died ten days later. As a result, Abigail became one of David's wives, and the story stands out as a classic example of a peacemaker's important role in society.

Abigail saw a conflict spinning out of control. She realized that the total annihilation of her family was at hand. She quickly went to work to promote peace and saw a better outcome as a result. David was stopped from doing something murderous in his rage, and Nabal was dealt with by the Lord for his foolishness ten days later. Abigail found a spot at the king's table as one of his wives. It is evident that being an active peacemaker turned her situation around for the better. Today, centuries later, millions still read her story of creative reconciliation. What a remarkable story it is!

Please know that, given our many differences, it is inevitable that there will be conflicts between people. It is in conflict where the peacemaker gets to shine. If someone in the room is willing to work towards peace, irreconcilable differences can be made bearable. Terms can be negotiated. Jesus, the Prince of Peace, declared that peacemakers would be called the children of God. It stands to reason that God's children are expected to be people who habitually work towards peace and harmony, and not division.

Scripture promises that joy will be the reward of those who promote peace:

> *Deceit is in the hearts of those who plot evil, but those who promote peace have joy.*

> — PROVERBS 12:20 (NIV)

David writes about the beauty of people coexisting in harmonious concert, in spite of their differences. He writes that God commands an extraordinary blessing on people who live together in such a blissful state:

> *How wonderful and pleasant it is when brothers live together in harmony! For harmony is as precious as the anointing oil that was poured over Aaron's head, that ran down his beard and onto the border of his robe. Harmony is as refreshing as the dew from Mount Hermon that falls on the mountains of Zion. And there the Lord has pronounced his blessing, even life everlasting.*

— PSALM 133 (NLT)

The word *harmony* is translated in other translations as *unity*. I do like to be blessed by God in my life. I would want to live in unity with my brothers and sisters. How about you?

Jesus promised a blessed life to peacemakers, to those who work towards peace. I want to encourage you to work towards peace among those you encounter. Work towards peace, even if it is a long process comprised of several difficult conversations. In the end, the Lord will command a blessing on the process and all the people who were willing to work towards peace. You are a child of God, so be a peacemaker!

ACTION STEPS:

1. Peace is a process. Peace is made, and it takes several steps.
2. To be a child of God means making peace with others, even when it is hard.
3. God blesses peacemakers.

4. Be a peacemaker. Ask the Lord to help you when it gets difficult.

5. Expect the Lord to give you favor in the peace process. Ask the Lord to command His blessing as you bring peace between divided people.

REVIEW:

1. God is a God of Peace.
2. Jesus Gave Us Peace With The Father.
3. Where God Rules Peace Is Evident.
4. Let Holy Spirit Control Your Mind.
5. Holy Spirit's Teachings Bring Peace.
6. Peace Is A Fruit Of The Spirit.
7. Peace Is A Blessing From The Lord.
8. Fix Your Thoughts On God And Obtain Peace.
9. Let Peace Rule Your Heart.
10. Love Peace.
11. Jesus' Words Bring Peace.
12. Peace of Mind and Heart.
13. Trusting God Leads To Peaceful Sleep.
14. There Is No Peace For The Wicked.
15. Doing Good Results In Peace.
16. Plan For Peace And Experience Joy.
17. Please God And Experience Peace With Your Enemies.
18. God's Children Are Peacemakers.

---

1. See 1 Samuel 25:1-44.

⑲

DON'T WORRY. PRAY. THEN PEACE WILL FOLLOW

> *Don't worry about anything; instead, pray about everything.*
> *Tell God what you need, and thank him for all he has*
> *done. Then you will experience God's peace, which exceeds*
> *anything we can understand. His peace will guard your*
> *hearts and minds as you live in Christ Jesus.*

— PHILIPPIANS 4:6-7 (NLT)

Paul instructed the Philippians that they were not supposed to worry about *anything*. Hold on a second! Did he really mean *anything*? Let's stop there and consider the ramifications of such an instruction. Surely we should worry about something! What about nuclear warfare, global warming, pestilences, famines, wars, obesity, and Christian persecution? Surely there must be something that we are allowed to worry about as believers! Come on Paul! Be reasonable!

Paul lived in tumultuous times. Believers were incarcerated, tortured and killed. They were executed in public arenas in horrible circumstances. He knew that his readers were worried about many things, but he wrote them to stop worrying. Why? Because worry doesn't change your reality and it steals your peace.

Prayer, not worry, is a much more productive activity to engage in when your world is falling apart. He wrote that they shouldn't worry about *anything*, but instead, pray about *everything*.

Put that negative energy into positive action. Talk to God about everything that comes up on your mental radar screen. Tell Him what you need and thank Him for what He has done. See the two parts of your conversation with God? Ask about your needs and thank Him for what He has done!

Gratitude alleviates the pangs of anxiety. After you have prayed and thanked the Lord for His faithfulness, you will experience God's peace. This very same peace will subsequently act as a holy doorman. Peace will keep the worries of this world from entering your heart and minds as you live in Christ Jesus.

It is so easy just to read over this scripture and miss the sequence of events. First, you decide to stop worrying. Second, you bring your concerns to God in prayer. Third, you thank God for His faithfulness in the past. Fourth, you are bathed in a peace that can only come from spending time with the Lord. You know that He will be faithful in the future as well. Fifth, that peace shelters you from the storms of life.

You can live a peaceful life when you stop worrying and start praying. Know this: God is for you and not against you. His peace can shield you from life's most complicated worries.

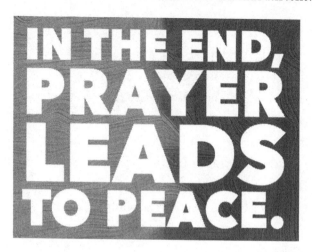

ACTION STEPS:

1. Don't worry about anything. Not. A. Thing.
2. Start praying about everything.
3. Ask God for His provision and thank Him with a heart filled with gratitude for His provisions to date.
4. Welcome the resulting peace and watch it shelter you from life's many worries.

REVIEW:

1. God is a God of Peace.
2. Jesus Gave Us Peace With The Father.
3. Where God Rules Peace Is Evident.
4. Let Holy Spirit Control Your Mind.

5. Holy Spirit's Teachings Bring Peace.

6. Peace Is A Fruit Of The Spirit.

7. Peace Is A Blessing From The Lord.

8. Fix Your Thoughts On God And Obtain Peace.

9. Let Peace Rule Your Heart.

10. Love Peace.

11. Jesus' Words Bring Peace.

12. Peace of Mind and Heart.

13. Trusting God Leads To Peaceful Sleep.

14. There Is No Peace For The Wicked.

15. Doing Good Results In Peace.

16. Plan For Peace And Experience Joy.

17. Please God And Experience Peace With Your Enemies.

18. God's Children Are Peacemakers.

19. Don't Worry. Pray. Then Peace Will Follow.

20

BE AT PEACE WITH OTHERS

> *Make every effort to keep yourselves united in the Spirit, binding yourselves together with peace. For there is one body and one Spirit, just as you have been called to one glorious hope for the future.*

— EPHESIANS 4:3-6 (NLT)

I like the word *effort* in this scripture because it is a realistic assessment of what it takes to stay united and connected within the Body of Christ. In the best of times, that unity is a fragile thing that should be handled very carefully. One word out of place can disturb the peace that defines a group of people. One simple and seemingly insignificant misunderstanding can unravel a carefully constructed unity.

The apostle Peter wrote in his letter to the churches to underscore this reality:

> *If you want to enjoy life and see many happy days, keep your*

tongue from speaking evil and your lips from telling lies. Turn away from evil and do good. Search for peace, and work to maintain it. The eyes of the Lord watch over those who do right, and his ears are open to their prayers. But the Lord turns his face against those who do evil.

— 1 PETER 3:10-12 (NLT)

We all can tell stories of how a rumor or misinformation tore a beautiful family apart with dire consequences for all involved. Peter cautioned his readers to search for peace, implying that at times it may be missing. Put in the work it takes to maintain peace.

Why is that important? Peter reminds us that the Lord watches over His people and that He listens to the prayers of those who do right. The Lord does not receive those who do evil. What does the Lord consider to be evil, then?

In the Book of Wisdom, Proverbs, the writer listed what God hates as a cautionary reminder to his readers:

> *There are six things the Lord hates—no, seven things he detests: haughty eyes, a lying tongue, hands that kill the innocent, a heart that plots evil, feet that race to do wrong, a false witness who pours out lies, a person who sows discord in a family.*

— PROVERBS 6:16-19 (NLT)

When you consider this list, it is clear that creating discord will warrant God's fiercest opposition. Almost everything on the list is contrary to a peaceful existence and brings about division.

On the other hand, when you work hard to be at peace with others in the family of God, you will enjoy God's favor. Your prayers will be answered. Isn't that what you want?

Make every effort to remain in a state of peace and work diligently towards peace when it is lost.

ACTION STEPS:

1. Pay attention to the level of peace in your relationships. If peace is absent, investigate and start the process towards restoring it.
2. Watch your words. They have the power to lessen the peace you experience in your life.
3. Don't sow discord in the family. God hates it, and your prayers will not be heard.
4. Work hard at being at peace with others because that will provide you with many joyful days in your life!

REVIEW:

1. God is a God of Peace.
2. Jesus Gave Us Peace With The Father.
3. Where God Rules Peace Is Evident.
4. Let Holy Spirit Control Your Mind.
5. Holy Spirit's Teachings Bring Peace.
6. Peace Is A Fruit Of The Spirit.
7. Peace Is A Blessing From The Lord.
8. Fix Your Thoughts On God And Obtain Peace.
9. Let Peace Rule Your Heart.
10. Love Peace.
11. Jesus' Words Bring Peace.
12. Peace of Mind and Heart.
13. Trusting God Leads To Peaceful Sleep.
14. There Is No Peace For The Wicked.
15. Doing Good Results In Peace.
16. Plan For Peace And Experience Joy.
17. Please God And Experience Peace With Your Enemies.
18. God's Children Are Peacemakers.
19. Don't Worry. Pray. Then Peace Will Follow.
20. Keep The Peace With Others.

21

LIVE IN PEACE AND HARMONY WITH OTHERS

> *Dear brothers and sisters, I close my letter with these last words: Be joyful. Grow to maturity. Encourage each other. Live in harmony and peace. Then the God of love and peace will be with you.*

— II CORINTHIANS 13:11 (NLT)

Paul closed his letter to the Corinthians with those words. As we are in our last chapter together on this topic of peace, allow me to echo his words. Think about what makes the Lord of love and peace feel welcome among us. Paul tells us to live in harmony and peace as we encourage each other. He tells us to be joyful and to grow to maturity.

Mature people are joyful and hopeful regardless of circumstances. They choose to live up, instead of down. They lift others, even as the Lord lifts them. They decide to live harmoniously and at peace with each other. They know that our differences are divinely orchestrated. Each one can make their unique contribution and have value in the Body of Christ.

It is a mature approach to see that people are different from us and still celebrate and encourage them. How often we lose our peace with others because we insist that they do as we prefer. If they are designed differently, they will also do things differently:

United Worship: A Fragrant Offering Ascending To The Heavens.
(Acrylics on canvas by Iann Schonken, 2014)

The human body has many parts, but the many parts make up one whole body. So it is with the body of Christ. Some of us are Jews, some are Gentiles, some are slaves, and some are free. But we have all been baptized into one body by one Spirit, and we all share the same Spirit. Yes, the body has many different parts, not just one part. If the foot says, 'I am not a part of the body because I am not a hand,' that does not make it any less a part of the body. And if the ear says, 'I am not part of the body because I am not an eye,' would that make it any less a part of the body? If the whole body were an eye, how would you hear? Or if your whole body were an ear, how would you smell anything? But our bodies have many parts, and God has put each part just where he wants it. How strange a body would be if it had only one part! Yes, there are many parts, but only one body. The eye can never say to the hand, 'I don't need you.' The head can't say to the feet, 'I don't need you.' In fact, some parts of the body that seem weakest and least important are actually the most necessary. And the parts we regard as less honorable are those we clothe with the greatest care. So we carefully protect those parts that should not be seen, while the more honorable parts do not require this special care. So God has put the body together such that extra honor and care are given to those parts that have less dignity. This makes for harmony among the members, so that all the members care for each other. If one part suffers, all the parts suffer with it, and if one part is honored, all the parts are glad. All of you together are Christ's body, and each of you is a part of it.

— I CORINTHIANS 12:12-27 (NLT)

We can get to a place where we are no longer offended when someone is different from us in perspective or function. We can be at peace knowing that there is more than enough opportunity for each one of us to make a beautiful contribution to the Kingdom of God. When we mature in this knowledge, we can live in harmony and peace. The Lord of love and peace will be welcomed in our midst.

Let's choose joy. Let's choose harmony and peace. Let's encourage others regardless of how different they are from us. Let's welcome the Lord of love and peace in a community of ever-increasing love and peace. As a result, you will be peaceful and joyful as you engage in the life-long art of peace!

ACTION STEPS:

1. Choose joy.
2. Choose to mature in your thinking about others.
3. Encourage others.
4. Live in harmony and peace.
5. Welcome the Lord of Peace in your every day.
6. Engage daily in the life-long art of peace!

REVIEW:

1. God is a God of Peace.
2. Jesus Gave Us Peace With The Father.
3. Where God Rules Peace Is Evident.
4. Let Holy Spirit Control Your Mind.
5. Holy Spirit's Teachings Bring Peace.
6. Peace Is A Fruit Of The Spirit.
7. Peace Is A Blessing From The Lord.
8. Fix Your Thoughts On God And Obtain Peace.
9. Let Peace Rule Your Heart.
10. Love Peace.
11. Jesus' Words Bring Peace.
12. Peace of Mind and Heart.
13. Trusting God Leads To Peaceful Sleep.
14. There Is No Peace For The Wicked.
15. Doing Good Results In Peace.
16. Plan For Peace And Experience Joy.
17. Please God And Experience Peace With Your Enemies.

18. God's Children Are Peacemakers.
19. Don't Worry. Pray. Then Peace Will Follow.
20. Keep The Peace With Others.
21. Live in Harmony and Peace.

APPENDIX 1

BIBLE TRANSLATIONS CITED:

AMP: *The Amplified Bible*
    Grand Rapids: Zondervan (1965).

LB: *Living Bible*
    Wheaton, IL: Tyndale House Publishers (1976).

NASB: *New American Standard Bible*
    Anaheim, CA: Foundation Press (1973).

NIV: *New International Version*
    Colorado Springs: Biblica, Inc. (1978, 1984).

NKJV: *New King James Version*
    Nashville. TN: Thomas Nelson (1982).

NLT: *New Living Translation*

Carol Stream, IL: Tyndale House Foundation (2015).

ABOUT THE AUTHOR

In 1988, Iann Schonken came to the United States from his country of birth, South Africa, to complete his theological studies. After receiving his master's Degree in Religion, he went on to assist various ministries in administrative duties, speaking and consultations. In 1996, Iann established his own non-profit organization and served his calling in the United States, Brazil, Mozambique, Madagascar, India, the Philippines, Israel, Canada, South Africa, Tanzania and Australia.

Iann has over thirty years of ministerial experience, including ten years as lead pastor in Oceanside, CA. He has authored several books and he currently serves on the executive leadership team at Visalia First, a congregation in Visalia, California. He has been married for over 28 years to his wife Melodi, and is the grateful father of three boys.

For his other books, art, resources and talks, check out his website at: www.iannschonken.com.